UNLEASH YOUR HIDDEN POKER
MEMORY

How to Win at Texas Hold'em
by Turning Your Brain into
a Poker Tracking Machine

BENNETT ONIKA

ECW PRESS

Published by ECW Press
2120 Queen Street East, Suite 200, Toronto, Ontario, Canada M4E IE2
416-694-3348 / info@ecwpress.com

LIBRARY AND ARCHIVES CANADA CATALOGUING IN PUBLICATION

Onika, Bennett
Unleash your hidden poker memory : how to win at Texas
hold'em by turning your brain into a poker tracking machine
/ Bennett Onika.

ISBN 978-1-77041-072-5
ALSO ISSUED AS: 978-1-77090-229-9 (PDF); 978-1-77090-230-5 (EPUB)

1. Poker. 2. Memory. 3. Mnemonics. I. Title.

GV1251.O55 2012   795.412   C2011-906945-8

Cover: Cyanotype
Type: Troy Cunningham
Printing: Friesens   1   2   3   4   5

The publication of *Unleash Your Hidden Poker Memory* has benefitted from the financial support of the Government of Canada through the Canada Book Fund for our publishing activities, and the contribution of the Government of Ontario through the Ontario Book Publishing Tax Credit. The marketing of this book was made possible with the support of the Ontario Media Development Corporation.

PRINTED AND BOUND IN CANADA

UNLEASH YOUR
HIDDEN POKER
MEMORY

CONTENTS

WARNING

If you read this book from cover to cover without taking the time to do the exercises properly, you might easily become overwhelmed. For best results, go through the chapters one by one and take the time to learn each concept well. Each day your memory will grow, but you must have faith. Take it one day at a time. If it takes you a few days to master a concept, so be it, but *do not* move on to another chapter until you have mastered the previous one. Training your memory will require work, but once you have the foundation built you will be amazed at how easily you can recall vast amounts of information. Enjoy.

PREFACE

As I write this, I am thinking about all the other prefaces I have ever read, about the person who felt compelled to put his or her thoughts on paper and what a spiritual experience writing the book was, and who wanted to change the world with his or her novel. I am going to be brutally honest. I put together an excellent program that combines the latest information on a brain's ability to recall information and my experiences at the poker table. I don't really care about being famous, nor do I really care if you — my future opponent — put the entire book to work. In fact, my biggest hope is that you buy this book and *don't* read it, because it will put a few bucks in my pocket from the royalties, and I won't have to worry about a truly difficult opponent the next time I'm in Las Vegas. Should you work on your memory as you work on your game, this book will help you to take your game to the next level. Where you previously used instinct to deduce how active a player might be, you will now be able to see players changing gears as if they are driving a bus, make a complete inventory of played hands in specific positions at the table, and instantly recall your win rate for your hand versus any random hole cards your opponent has based on how loosely or tightly she plays.

I would also like to point out that, though this book is basic when it comes to memory techniques, you should have a really good understanding of poker, both tournament and cash play, because the poker game itself will mostly be ignored. This is not a how-to-play-poker book but a book on how to train yourself to instantly recall vast amounts of information about your opponents and up-cards at the poker table. To my knowledge, no book has been written that combines an awakened powerful memory (which everyone has — yes, even you!) and how to use it to crush your opponents.

When I first heard of the sharp intellect and record of Stu Ungar, I wished I could be as good as he was. He is widely considered to be the best no-limit tournament player who ever lived and the greatest gin rummy player. He is also my inspiration for writing this book. What separated Stu from the field were his incredible memory skills. It was said he possessed an eidetic memory. Against Bob Stupak he bet he could count his way through a six-deck shoe and tell Stupak what the last card was. Stu won. At first, I thought it was impossible to play as well as Stu, mainly because I didn't have his eidetic memory. I found out later that your memory is like any other muscle in the body — the more you work it, the stronger it becomes. In short, if you don't have an eidetic memory, with the systems in this book you can get closer than you ever have. I can now count through a deck in less than two minutes and tell you what the last card is. I can memorize a shuffled deck in order in under nine minutes. With a little work, you will be able to as well.

One final thing — this book is a process. Treat each chapter as a learning module and master each one, because each chapter builds on the previous one. Make sure you understand all the concepts in each chapter and know them so well you could do the exercises in your sleep. The better you do this, the more success you will have. Also, if you do read the book cover to cover, don't get discouraged with the amount of information you see; everything I have written in this book is achievable by anyone, so come back and do the work — you will be glad you did.

I hope you find the information in this book valuable and profitable. Good luck.

CHAPTER T
UNLEARN WHAT YOU
HAVE LEARNED

I know what you are thinking. Chapter T? I am returning this book — it's horrible. Well, before you do, be advised that everything in this book has a purpose. As you will find out, there is a reason it is Chapter T and not Chapter 1. Before we delve into the real study part of the book, I need to eliminate any old myths you have about your brain and how you have been told it works. Your brain works vastly differently than you might think. All the reading I have done from the leading researchers on the way a "normal" brain works and how a memory is processed trumps anything any schoolteacher told me about studying. I was always told that studying and recalling information is hard and that you have to work at it. I am telling you right now: your memory is either trained or untrained. Once you train it, you will be able to remember more information than you ever thought possible.

Having made a wager or two, I am willing to bet that you were just like me before I trained my mind to remember things. In fact, I always knew I was a fairly bright guy: maybe not Einstein or Newton, but certainly smart enough to figure things out. I never had any trouble understanding the concepts teachers were teaching. I found school incredibly boring because teachers taught at an incredibly slow pace. Also, my parents always told me that studying was hard and tedious, that nothing worth learning and truly understanding was easy. To put it simply, I was just a horrible test taker. When it came time to remember things for a test, I was horrible at it. In fact, in grade 10, I had forgotten about a test on U.S. geography that tested us on the 50 states and their capitals and just found out about it that morning. I studied them as hard as I could for 20 minutes before the test and flunked it miserably. I think I got maybe 10 states and a few of their capitals right. I would have had to spend hours using rote memory even if I had known about the test in advance.

It bothered me so badly that, when I first learned the techniques for memorization, I wanted to have another chance at that 20-minute window. I memorized not only the 50 states and their capitals but also their slogans and *the order* in which they came. I did it in just 18 minutes. I was also able to recall the information in its entirety two days later without review. I was shocked at how easy it was.

I am telling you this not to brag about how great I am but to illustrate how easy it is to train yourself. In fact, I am proud that I can memorize a shuffled deck of cards in under 10 minutes. You might think that is amazing. Do you know that the world record is under 25 seconds? Now *that* is amazing.

Also amazing is that the average poker player will only have three to five pieces of information on you at the poker table — if he is lucky, seven or eight. He will also categorize you as a certain type of player and expect that, once he has "figured" you out, his work is done. He is loose passive and bets hard with top pair. When he flares his nostrils, he is bluffing.

Now you will be the extraordinary poker player. You will be the card player who has an encyclopedia of general bluffs and strong tells memorized. You will know the exact percentage of hands played by each opponent at the table. You will be able to memorize a catalog of hole cards played by all players at the table in each position played and whether they raised or limped. In Texas Hold'em, you will have all 169 hole cards memorized in rank — yes, you will know that K7 offsuit is ranked the 97th best hand out of 169. You will be able to store in your memory whatever you want for a live game of poker. You will be able to play a live tournament or cash game and have virtual computer knowledge on all your opponents while they question your raise in their heads and say, "Well, he hasn't raised in a while, he must have a hand."

To move forward, I am going to quote Yoda, one of my favorite Jedi masters from *Star Wars*: "You must unlearn what you have learned." Below are some myths you might believe; we are going to unlearn these myths and relearn new realities.

MYTH: My memory is what it is, and I will never be able to improve it.

REALITY: You are born with nearly 100 billion cells called neurons. When you learn, these neurons form pathways with other neurons — up to 10,000 pathways between each neuron. In short, your brain is the most complex computing system ever created and has incredible power. The more you work your brain, the more pathways will form, and your ability to recall information will become much better. Stop using your brain and eventually you die. Researchers have confirmed that, when you retire from work, you are far more likely to die sooner if you shut down and do nothing. If you volunteer or have a part-time business or job, you are far more likely to live a long and healthy life.

MYTH: You can't teach this old dog new tricks.

REALITY: Although you have a fixed number of neurons when you start out in life, you still have 90 percent of them by age 80. Your age can cause you a bit more of a time lag to recall the information, but the brain continues to form new pathways even after this age with the neurons that are left. With the right techniques, you can still train your memory to be effective whether you are 20 or 80.

MYTH: I have a photographic memory.

REALITY: Many researchers are now calling photographic memory a myth. That someone can look at something once and instantly remember every detail has rarely if ever been done. In fact, the world memory championships are won consistently by extraordinary people who have yet to claim photographic memory. Thus far, all have used memory-training techniques to develop their memories.

MYTH: I am not smart enough to do this.

REALITY: Unless you have a disease of the brain, your general knowledge is a function of your memory and ability to recall information. Think back to high school: all the best students were the best test takers who could remember concepts when they wanted to. In high school, was there ever a course on how to effectively memorize and recall the concepts? That course didn't exist for me. My system will not only help you to remember things for your life but also give you a tremendous advantage at the poker table. Moreover, most memory champions were average students at best before they learned their systems! In fact, Ben Pridmore, World Memory Champ from England (and also the person who memorized a shuffled deck in under 25 seconds), to this day frequently misplaces his keys and forgets names if he isn't concentrating on them. Yet he memorized pi to 50,000 digits!

MYTH: This system of memory is a lot of work.
REALITY: In the beginning, it will seem that way because, to memorize the first few ideas, you have a brain not used to remembering items. As your mind is trained and forms more pathways, your ability to recall information will become easier, and you will have less work in memorizing huge quantities of information.

In the words of Henry Ford, "Whether you think you can, or think you can't, either way you are right." If you believe in yourself and work at this, you will achieve a skill that few people in the world have and even fewer in the poker world.

For your first assignment, I have a basic memory test for you. I would like you to take out a deck of cards and shuffle them. Once you have shuffled them, pull 10 cards out of the deck without looking at them and then go through the other 42 cards, looking at them one by one and trying to remember all of the cards that have been played. Take as long as you want to go through the deck, but remember to write down the time. Now see if you can list all 10 cards that you originally pulled out of the deck. Now, if that seems too hard, write down "Way too hard!" Or you could start with just one suit and shuffle the 13 cards and pull one out. Now try to remember just the last card that wasn't played. Whatever test you do, write it down along with the date and time spent.

Now I want you to put the 10 cards back into the deck and shuffle it up. Go through the entire deck, looking at each card, and try to remember all of the cards in sequence. Again take as much time as you need and write down how many you get correct in a row as well as how long it took you and the date you did it.

If that's too hard, try just 10 cards in sequence and write down how long it took you. Come back in 25 minutes and see if you can still remember them in order.

Write your results here:

The reason for these exercises now is that I want you to be blown away by your ability to remember sequences and information. You will look back on the numbers you see above and think, "I can't believe how fast I am." I know what I said: "That's incredible!" I want you to look back on your results in awe of your newfound sense of recall. Once you see that your brain is the most powerful computer ever created, and believe you can memorize even the most complicated information quickly and easily, it won't be long before you have the confidence to memorize bigger amounts of information, which will help you to take down any opponent — pro or amateur — you face at any major tournament in the world.

You now know your brain is an incredibly powerful computer capable of amazing feats of recall. You are also likely skeptical at this point of your own abilities. Let's move on and make you a believer.

CHAPTER N
THE BUILDING BLOCKS
OF MEMORIZATION

Everyone has heard the saying "A picture is worth a thousand words." Well, in memory training, nothing is closer to the truth. I would argue that one picture is worth more than any couple of paragraphs of description. *The ultimate building block of memorization is pictures.* If you are going to succeed in this endeavor, you must understand that every abstract thing you see can easily be remembered if you turn it into a picture.

A study conducted in 1973 showed 10,000 images to average people over five days, and then they were immediately tested on which images they recalled seeing. Over 80% of the images were recalled accurately. This test showed that we as humans have an acute sense of perception. What is better is if you close your eyes and visualize a picture: your brain cannot tell the difference between an image you actually saw and one you visualized. To your brain, it is all the same. In contrast, it is harder to remember abstract things. Numbers, letters, words, and playing cards all fall into this category. That's why we catch ourselves on four flushes checking what suit our card is. We know it's red, but is it a diamond or a heart? We wouldn't have this problem if we played with a four-color deck since each suit would have its own color.

This chapter focuses on turning everything you find abstract into a vivid image. It is important to note that, the more ridiculous your image is, the easier it will be to remember. Let me give you an example. What were you doing September 10, 2001? What about September 11, 2001? I would be willing to bet you can remember exactly what you were doing on the 11th versus the 10th right down to the slightest detail. September 10th you probably have little idea because it was an ordinary day. September 11th was a day of disaster that cemented what you were doing that day into your long-term memory. Every detail right down to the smell of the cup of coffee you might have had is forever ingrained in your long-term memory due to the emotional upheaval of that day.

Let's try to use this knowledge in everyday life. When you try to recall something, create emotionally charged, weird images, and you will remember them no problem. If you want to remember where you last placed your keys, the next time you put your keys down picture them exploding and not only blowing your hand off but also putting a gaping hole in your expensive oak table. Try to forget that image. When I go to the mall, I look at colors and images in the parking lot. Then I pretend my car is affected by them, so when I think of my car later I think of the image and color. For instance, the last time I parked it was *Nevada green*. So I pictured my green car smashing into the sign on the Las Vegas Strip. Then, after it crashed, a whole bunch of green slime oozed out of it. *Give your brain a picture it can't forget, and remembering will be easier.*

The first thing we are going to do is equate the first 10 numbers with the 10 basic sounds in the English language. Each sound has an assigned number. We want to easily interchange a sound for a number, so if we have two numbers we want to turn them into an image using the sounds we have. An example is 4154. For 4 we have an *R* sound, 1 is a *T* sound (hence Chapter T), and 5 is an *L* sound. For this number, I have picked the image of a *retailer*. So now, if you want to remember the number, you remember RETAILER; every sound in the word tells you what number it is in order. RTLR or 4154. If you don't like retailer, you can use RAT LURE or IRATE LIAR — whatever you want — just make sure the RTLR are in order. Don't ask me how or why T is 1 and 5 is L, but they seem to be the standard for all memory training.

So you can know the sounds and their associated numbers, I have provided an easy way to remember them. If these images do not work for you, find ones that do work after you have read this book and developed your memory. In the meantime, learn these images as well as you can — they are the building blocks for future knowledge. I call them your body of base knowledge. Why? Because I place them on your body *in order*. That way it is easier to memorize them. This system was created a long time ago and is called the LOCI method. The ancient Romans created it to make their speeches easier to remember by placing key ideas on specific places in their villages. They would associate an image with a topic in the speech and then with a particular building. For example, if they had a speech on horses and carriages, and the first topic was wheel redesign, they would picture a huge wheel on their house, the first place they left in the morning. Then perhaps it was the hitch attached to the horse they wanted to talk about, so in their minds they would associate a hitch with the next stop, which might be the blacksmith, and so on. Then they would simply "walk through" the rest of their village and see the objects on the buildings to bring up the next topics. This is an easy way to remember things in order.

In this case, it will be your body. Let's start at your toes.

1 = T/D for toes

2 = N for knee (starts with a K but sounds like an N, so don't worry about the K)

3 = M for muscle (use your quadriceps on your leg)

4 = R for rear end

5 = L for liver

6 = SH or J or CH for shoulder

7 = hard C for collarbone

8 = F or V for forehead

9 = B or P for bald spot (top of your head)

0 = soft C for ceiling

This phonetic alphabet has been well documented in several memory books, notably *The Memory Book* by Harry Lorayne, and on the Internet by several authors, as well as Remember Media's remember playing cards. You require this training as a precursor to applying the systems later.

Again, I'm not sure how or why these particular sounds were associated with these particular numbers, but any reading and research I have done on the mind and memory have the same sounds associated with the same numbers. I can't stress enough how important it is to know these sounds like the back of your hand — they should come as automatically as breathing. I would practice by writing out numbers with two to four digits and then converting them into images and back again. When you become adept at this, move on to the next chapter.

In review, we know that the brain thinks in pictures and that stronger emotions are tied to those memories that are stored. And we have memorized the 10 basic sounds in the English language and associated them with numbers.

EXERCISES

Convert these sentences into a list of numbers.

    1. Your brain thinks in pictures.

    2. You have one hundred billion neurons.

    3. Train your memory every day.

    4. You have a super memory.

    5. I can memorize a shuffled deck of cards in order.

Create words out of the following numbers.

    6. 4581

    7. 267

    8. 9364

    9. 1548

    10. 7632

CHAPTER M

EACH CARD HAS AN IMAGE

Now that you have an expert grasp of the sounds associated with the numbers, we will move on to the next phase of your memory training. This involves putting a specific image on a particular card in a deck of cards. We will turn each card into an image you can easily recognize. It will be easy to start to remember each image because we will derive the image from the letter associated with each card.

For example, every heart in the deck will start with the letter H, every club with C, every diamond with D, and finally every spade with S. Aces will be our number 1 cards, and each numbered card will be its value. 10 cards will be a 0 or soft *C* sound. Jacks will be numbered 11 because they are the 11th card, Queens 12, and Kings 13. Each number will have a specific letter associated with it.

Let's start with hearts in the table below.

ACE OF HEARTS	H	T/D	HAT, HUT
2 OF HEARTS	H	N	HEN, HUN
3 OF HEARTS	H	M	HAM, HOME
4 OF HEARTS	H	R	HAIR, HARE
5 OF HEARTS	H	L	HAIL, HULA, HALL, HELL

6 OF HEARTS	H	SH/CH	HITCH, HUTCH
7 OF HEARTS	H	K	HICK, HOOK
8 OF HEARTS	H	F/V	HOOF, HIVE
9 OF HEARTS	H	P/B	HIP, HOOP
10 OF HEARTS	H	S/C	HOSE, HAZE
JACK OF HEARTS	H	TT	HOT TEA, HUTTED
QUEEN OF HEARTS	H	TN	HOT KNEE, HAY TEN
KING OF HEARTS	H	TM	HIGH DOME, HOT DAME

Although the images vary slightly, this system has been used by Remember Media's remember playing cards as well as several other Internet authors. It has also been documented by Harry Lorayne in *The Memory Book*, though he uses different images.

So you see there is a method to the madness. Each card has a specific sound associated with each number, and when you first start learning the images you will likely find yourself thinking about the letters to give you clues to the images. That is fine. But study the images so well that, when you see a 3 of hearts, you instantly think of a big juicy HAM. Also make sure that it is an image and not an action. For example, it must be a HUT you are visualizing and not a HIT. It must be an object when you start out, for you will have an easier time remembering an image versus an action. Your speed in recalling the images will go a long way toward collecting information at the poker table.

Here is a list of the image I use for each card.

AH	HUT		AC	CAT
2H	HEN		2C	CANE
3H	HAM		3C	COMB
4H	HARE		4C	CAR
5H	HAIL		5C	COAL
6H	HITCH		6C	CASH
7H	HOOK		7C	CAKE

8H	HIVE		8C	COFFEE	
9H	HOOP		9C	COP	
TH	HOSE		TC	CASE	
JH	HOT TEA		JC	CADET	
QH	HAY TEN		QC	COTTON	
KH	HIGH DOME		KC	CUT ME (*Rocky*)	
AD	DIET		AS	SUIT	
2D	DEAN		2S	SUN	
3D	DIME		3S	SUMO	
4D	DOOR		4S	SOUR (GRAPES)	
5D	DOLL		5S	SAIL	
6D	DISH		6S	SUSHI	
7D	DOCK		7S	SOCK	
8D	DIVE		8S	SOFA	
9D	DIAPER		9S	SOAP	
TD	DICE		TS	SAUCE	
JD	DOTTED		JS	STEED	
QD	DAYTONA		QS	STAIN	
KD	DAYTIMER		KS	STEM	

These exercises might not seem like they will immediately help your poker game, but I assure you that in the long run they will. When I first started, my memory wasn't trained, and I found it difficult to picture certain images. The longer I worked at it, the more I found myself increasing my abilities daily. I often smiled at my progress, as I'm sure you will at yours. I could almost see the pathways forming in my brain as I recalled more and more information. These building blocks will train your mind, just as doing math questions in school trained your math skills.

If you have a computer, you'll want to know that I have shared all my memory flashcards on a program called Flashcards Deluxe on my wonderful wife Leissa's iPad. I thank Leissa for letting me monopolize her birthday present! My cards are all there along with the images. The images vary from what I have written here, but feel free to download any of my flashcards for memory work you want to do. But I should warn readers that some of the cards contain images suitable only for mature audiences.

You should be able to rattle off these images in less than 45 seconds. Take a deck and start practicing. The first time I tried it, not only did it take me up to 10 minutes to get all the images, but I also got many of them wrong. Each time you review you get better, so work on it every day. Remember that your mind thinks in images, and the bigger and better your picture is, the easier it will be to do the exercises.

We have learned that every card has an image associated with it so that we don't become confused over the abstract nature of the card and in turn remember it easily. You now also know that each image is derived from the letter or letters associated with the number and suit of each card. On the next page are some exercises for you to practice.

EXERCISES

Convert the following decks.

1	DOCK
2	HIGH DOME
3	SOCK
4	COFFEE
5	CAR
6	COMB
7	HARE
8	HAY TEN
9	HUT
10	DEAN
11	CANE
12	DIME
13	STEM
14	COTTON
15	HAM
16	DAYTONA
17	SOAP
18	CADET
19	SUIT
20	SUN
21	DIET
22	COAL

1	3H
2	2C
3	7S
4	9D
5	8C
6	QC
7	AC
8	2H
9	TD
10	3D
11	7D
12	TC
13	QD
14	6D
15	9C
16	8D
17	9S
18	KD
19	QS
20	JS
21	3C
22	2S

23	DAYTIMER		23	5S
24	SAUCE		24	5H
25	CASH		25	4H
26	HOOK		26	9H
27	HITCH		27	JH
28	COAL		28	AD
29	HOT TEA		29	KS
30	SUSHI		30	2D
31	DIVE		31	8H
32	HEN		32	7H
33	DOOR		33	5D
34	SUMO		34	5C
35	SOUR (GRAPES)		35	6C
36	DOLL		36	4C
37	COP		37	TS
38	DIAPER		38	6H
39	DICE		39	4S
40	CAT		40	7C
41	DISH		41	3S
42	HOSE		42	JC
43	HOOP		43	4D
44	CAKE		44	QH
45	SOFA		45	6S
46	HIVE		46	JD
47	DOTTED		47	TH

48	CUT ME (*Rocky*)
49	STEED
50	STAIN
51	HAIL
52	CASE

48	KC
49	8S
50	KH
51	AH
52	AS

CHAPTER R
THE DESTRUCTION METHOD

Now that you are fluent in the art of card imagery, we get to the fun part. I am going to show you a system that will be great for any card game that has cards exposed. So in any stud game, bridge or even gin rummy, you will be able to instantly remember if that card has been played.

This method of knowing which card has been played is often called the *destruction* or *mutilation* method. Remember Media as well as Harry Lorayne in *The Memory Book* have referred to this method. We use it to destroy cards in stud games as well as keep track of VPIP later. It takes the images for the cards you have just learned and mutilates or destroys them in some way that is memorable. My favorites are pretending I am the mythical Medusa and turning the image into stone with my stare, and having my lightsaber from *Star Wars* and cutting the images into many pieces with the edges still red hot from the cuts.

The following is an exercise I did every day when I started and now do every two to three days just to stay sharp. I always try to cut down the time it takes for me to get through the deck.

1. Shuffle a deck of cards; then take out 10 cards and put them off to the side. Don't look at the cards.

2. Take the remaining deck and flip the first card, noting

the image you learned for the card in the previous
chapter.

3. When you see the card and the corresponding image,
   mutilate the image in some way that causes you to have
   an emotional response. When you see the 8 of hearts,
   you see a hive of hornets. Perhaps you take a sword and
   slice it in half but are stung 100 times.

4. Continue through the deck one by one, mutilating each
   card. Remember: the better your emotional response, the
   better you will remember that you mutilated the card.

5. Once you have completed the deck, systematically
   go through each card in order and recall if you have
   mutilated the image in some way. The cards you did
   not mutilate should stand out in your mind as if a light
   went off in your head. Those are the cards that have not
   been played.

To illustrate the method further, we will go through a couple of examples. One of my favorite mutilations is to take a sword and slice the image.
I have shuffled a deck of cards, and I want you to slice the images with me,
and let's see if we can deduce 10 cards that have been removed from the deck.

AD	DIET	Imagine yourself slicing through a tape measure and chopping it up.
4H	HARE	See yourself slicing off the head of a hare.
JC	CADET	Imagine cutting a Marine Corp cadet in half or his head off.
JD	DOTTED	Imagine cutting a polkadotted dress in half.
QS	STAIN	Cut a stain on your shirt in half — see it.
AH	HUT	Cut a giant hut into pieces.
KD	DAYTIMER	Cut your daytimer into pieces and cry because your meetings are gone.

9C	COP	Imagine a cop being sliced in half.
4S	SOUR (GRAPES)	Cut a sour grape in half and some of the juice hits your eye.
5S	SAIL	Cut your sail on your boat in half.
7S	SOCK	Cut your sock into shreds.
6C	CASH	Take a million dollars cash and cut it into shreds.
KC	CUT ME	Imagine the scene from *Rocky* and cut Rocky's eyes open.
9D	DIAPER	Cut a diaper in half and imagine all the number two falling out.
TC	CASE	Cut in half a briefcase containing your important documents.
TD	DICE	You are in Vegas playing craps, and you cut the dice in half.
3S	SUMO	A sumo wrestler is coming to flatten you, and you cut his head off.
KH	HIGH DOME	You cut the White House dome off, and the secret service arrests you.
5H	HAIL	Cut all the hailstones raining down in half.
7C	CAKE	Imagine slicing up a cake until it is mushy.
2D	DEAN	Imagine meeting James Dean and cutting his head off.
2S	SUN	You are on a rocket, and you slice the sun in half, and it goes dark.
TH	HOSE	You cut up your garden hose, and your lawn dies.
6D	DISH	You slice your wife's favorite dish, and she is mad at you for a week.
KS	STEM	You cut a rose stem in your wife's mouth.

8C	COFFEE	Slice up a huge bag of coffee beans, and they spill onto the floor.
7H	HOOK	You cut Captain Hook's hook off, and he can't hurt you anymore.
QH	HAY TEN	You slice up 10 bales of hay.
8H	HIVE	You cut a hornets' hive in half and get stung 100 times.
9S	SOAP	Cut the soap in your shower in half.
4C	CAR	You get a new Ferrari, and you cut it in half.
3D	DIME	You take a dime and cut it in half.
3H	HAM	You are at your family dinner, and you cut up the ham too small.
QC	COTTON	Cut a huge bale of cotton candy in half.
6H	HITCH	You cut your hitch into pieces.
AS	SUIT	You cut your Armani suit in half.
8S	SOFA	Slice your sofa in half.
2C	CANE	You see a person walking with a cane, and you cut it and watch her fall.
TS	SAUCE	You cut your mom's sauce up, and it makes a mess.
5D	DOLL	You cut up your daughter's favorite doll and make her cry.
QD	DAYTONA	You cut all the Daytona cars in half and ruin the race.
3C	COMB	You slice your sister's favorite comb in half.

Okay, now that you have all the images in your head, let's walk through them one by one and see which ones we didn't cut up. Let's start with hearts. Did we cut up a . . . ?

HUT	YES	SUIT	YES	CAT	NO	DIET	YES
HEN	NO	SUN	YES	CANE	YES	DEAN	YES
HAM	YES	SUMO	YES	COMB	YES	DIME	YES
HARE	YES	SOUR (GRAPES)	YES	CAR	YES	DOOR	NO
HAIL	YES	SAIL	YES	COAL	NO	DOLL	YES
HITCH	YES	SUSHI	NO	CASH	YES	DISH	YES
HOOK	YES	SOCK	YES	CAKE	YES	DOCK	NO
HIVE	YES	SOFA	YES	COFFEE	YES	DIVE	NO
HOOP	NO	SOAP	YES	COP	YES	DIAPER	YES
HOSE	YES	SAUCE	YES	CASE	YES	DICE	YES
HOT TEA	NO	STEED	NO	CADET	YES	DOTTED	YES
HAY TEN	YES	STAIN	YES	COTTON	YES	DAYTONA	YES
HIGH DOME	YES	STEM	YES	CUT ME	YES	DAYTIMER	YES

So the missing cards in the deck are 2H, 9H, JH, 6S, JS, AC, 5C, 4D, 7D, 8D. Now, if you didn't remember, then your image wasn't strong enough; if you got most of them, then it is a matter of practice and time before you will recall cards that have been played or not. The first time I did it and remembered each of the cards for a buddy of mine (Jack), he was quite impressed, and I was elated. Of course, had I screwed it up, I never would have heard the end of it, but it turned out to be an excellent exercise.

Now I want you to go back to the beginning of the book and check the date of your first results for this exercise. I think you will find you have trained your brain to remember far more quickly and accurately than at first with no techniques.

Your goal for this chapter is to run through a deck of cards in less than two minutes with 10 cards out and systematically and correctly name each card. Master this skill before you move on to the next chapter.

You can now take a deck of cards and use the destruction method to mutilate the images you have associated with the cards, and by doing so you will know which cards have been played.

EXERCISES

Go through the following three decks using a different destruction method for each deck and mentally determine which cards are left in each deck.

1	2	3
5H	6H	TC
9D	KD	7C
6D	3D	QC
9S	2D	AD
3S	TD	3H
8S	8D	6S
QS	8H	4D
AC	5C	QS
QD	4S	KC
JH	6C	5C
TH	TS	AH
2H	7H	TH
8D	AC	5S
9C	QD	7S
5D	7D	TD
KS	AS	4S
2C	JC	8H
AD	JS	6H
4C	6S	3C
QH	4H	5D

AH	3C	KD
5S	TC	2H
7S	5H	3S
6H	9D	3D
KH	KC	4C
3H	AD	4H
8C	2C	AC
3D	6D	QD
2D	9H	8D
TD	KH	6C
5C	2S	JH
7H	9C	9H
AS	TH	QH
2S	5S	8S
JS	7S	JD
4D	JH	5H
7C	3S	9D
6C	8S	2S
KD	9S	9C
7D	3H	8C
4H	4C	KH
3C	QH	JS

CHAPTER L
THE LOCATION OR LOCI METHOD

Great, now that you are a master of the destruction method, I will show you my way of memorizing a deck in sequence using the LOCI method. This method has been used by Harry Lorayne in *The Memory Book* and by Ron White in the Memory in a Month program. You will use the card images as well as the LOCI method in the VPIP method for analyzing loose versus rock-type players later. This is just another building block in your process.

To use the LOCI method, you must first determine the locations specific to you. I will give you mine as an example, and you can create yours. I have 10 rooms plus outdoor locations that give me 60 places where I can store images. This is ample for a 52-card deck. Each room has five distinct objects with which I can associate the images for the cards we have learned in the previous chapters.

The first room in my house when you walk in is my living room, and it has (in clockwise order) my couch, my coffee table, my padded bench, my fireplace, and my kids' toy storage unit. Make sure, when you create your locations to store information, that you do so in order and clockwise so you can readily see what comes next without thinking. Your job for this exercise is to find 10 rooms with five big objects in each and to make sure none of the objects is similar. My second room is the kitchen, and again in clockwise order it contains the fridge, stove, sink, kitchen table, and pantry. After the five rooms upstairs, I continue to the basement and have five rooms down there where I place things in my mind. Now, if you really wanted to, you could have 10 things per room, or seven, whatever works for you. I recommend having an easy number to multiply with so that, if someone asks you what the 43rd card is, you don't have to count all the way up — all you do is count by room. You could also have all 10 rooms on one floor, though I recommend splitting them up by five or 10 things so you can easily count up or down when finding an object or card in this case.

After you have 10 rooms completed with all of your objects, run through them a few times to make sure you have them all. If you have visualized your house well and have all of your objects in order, then it should be no problem to recall them. The last two items can be your front door and your back door.

Okay, once you have all of your rooms and all of your objects in them, shuffle a deck of cards and visually place each image for each card where your first object is in each room. I deal out five cards at once and place each object in each place.

To illustrate the process, I have shuffled a deck and listed my places below.

COUCH	HOOP
COFFEE TABLE	HIVE
PADDED BENCH	CANE
FIREPLACE	DOCK
TOY CHEST	SUN

Then I run back to number one and up to number five.

FRIDGE	STAIN
STOVE	DIAPER
SINK	SOUR GRAPES
KITCHEN TABLE	DIME
PANTRY	CASH

Then I run back to number one and up to number 10.

PAINTING	CAT
COMPUTER TABLE	CASE
ARMOIRE	SAUCE
BOOKSHELF	HAM
LIGHTSABERS	DIVE

Then I run back to number five and up to number 15.

CHANGE TABLE	HUT
CRIB	CADET
ROCKER	HIGH DOME
MEASURING DEVICE	SOAP
CROSS	SAIL

Again I run through the last 10 backward and forward; repeat this process to keep it in your memory every five cards you learn.

TV	DOOR
DRESSER	HOOK
LAMPS	HOSE
BED	COTTON
CLOSET	HITCH

Review:

FREEZER	HOT TEA
WASHER	HAIL
DRYER	STEED
FRIDGE	DOLL
STORAGE CLOSET	DAYTONA

♥

♣

♦

Review:

UPPER SHELF	DICE
RACK	HAY TEN
FLOOR	DAYTIMER
SOMBRERO	SUIT
PALM TREE	SOFA

Review:

POKER TABLE	CAKE
DVD SHELF	DISH
LOVE SEAT	SUMO
BIG SCREEN	DIET
SMALL TV	CUT ME

Review:

TOILET	SOCK
SINK	COAL
MIRROR	COMB
LIGHT	DEAN
TOWEL RACK	STEM

Review:

KENNEL	SUSHI
OUTLET	HARE
BED	CAT
INDENT	COFFEE
CABLE	CAR
ENTRANCE CLOSET	DOTTED
ENTRANCE	HEN

If you have visualized each image, you should be able to recite them in order. If you can't remember a place, mentally walk through each card. The right one will pop into your mind if you review it. The more you work on this, the faster you will become, and you will be amazed at how well you can recall the images. I have found that, if I do it too many times, I can actually get mixed up from the images I had the night before!

Now go back to the beginning of the book with these results and see how much more accurate you were in recalling the deck (and likely in much less time). If it was as significant as mine was the first time, you won't be able to let go of this book until you have mastered every system.

Make sure you remember the locations you have created at this point, because you will use them later. I have split my locations into five rooms each — my upper and lower house locations for 25 each when I use this method at the poker table. They are seats three and four always. I will go through the other positions later in the book.

For now, to build your ability to recall, try to do this exercise once every other night and try to get your time down under 10 minutes to memorize a deck. When you can memorize the deck effortlessly, move on to the next chapter.

You can now amaze your friends by memorizing a deck in sequence using the LOCI method.

EXERCISES

Let's take the decks from the last chapters and memorize them in order. Record your time each time and try to become faster. When you are done the first deck, cover it up and write your results in the column beside it. Compare your answers.

I		2		3	
5H		6H		TC	
9D		KD		7C	
6D		3D		QC	
9S		2D		AD	
3S		TD		3H	
8S		8D		6S	
QS		8H		4D	
AC		5C		QS	
QD		4S		KC	
JH		6C		5C	
TH		TS		AH	
2H		7H		TH	
8D		AC		5S	
9C		QD		7S	
5D		7D		TD	
KS		AS		4S	
2C		JC		8H	
AD		JS		6H	
4C		6S		3C	
QH		4H		5D	
AH		3C		KD	
5S		TC		2H	
7S		5H		3S	

6H		9D		3D	
KH		KC		4C	
3H		AD		4H	
8C		2C		AC	
3D		6D		QD	
2D		9H		8D	
TD		KH		6C	
5C		2S		JH	
7H		9C		9H	
AS		TH		QH	
2S		5S		8S	
JS		7S		JD	
4D		JH		5H	
7C		3S		9D	
6C		8S		2S	
KD		9S		9C	
7D		3H		8C	
4H		4C		KH	
3C		QH		JS	
TC		7C		2C	
JC		8C		JC	
QC		QC		2D	
KC		4D		6D	
JD		5D		7D	
8H		JD		7H	
9H		AH		AS	
4S		2H		9S	
6S		QS		TS	
TS		KS		KS	

CHAPTER SH, CH, OR J

169 IMAGES, ONE FOR EACH NUMBER

The next phase of your training involves putting images to numbers. Each number will be made to represent an image derived from the number itself. Learning these images is crucial for several things in poker. You will learn more places to keep track of the players' hands vis-à-vis how many hands have been dealt, giving you instant knowledge of a player's activity at the table or VPIP: *v*oluntarily *p*ut money *i*nto the *p*ot. You will also learn each set of hole cards' individual rank, which can keep you more disciplined in long sessions of poker. After all, K2 suited might look pretty after several hours or if you haven't played a hand in a while, but if you refer to it as hand number 65 out of 169 it might look less appealing to you. This is especially true against a player who has played three hands out of her last 20, putting her at 15% VPIP, her worst probable hand being 25th or 26th in rank (A8 suited or Q9 suited respectively).

Below is my list of numbers with the associated images you must learn. I have put in bold the letters of the first few images so you can see how we derive the images from the basic sounds you learned in Chapter T. You'll notice I have listed them up to 169 — the exact number of starting hands in Texas Hold'em. You guessed correctly: we will associate each image with an image of a starting hand, giving you an instant, computer-like knowledge of the rank of hand you have when starting off in Texas Hold'em. Numbers

0–100 are similar to those in Harry Lorayne's *The Memory Book*; I created numbers 101–69 using systems similar to those in *The Memory Book*.

#	IMAGE	#	IMAGE	#	IMAGE	#	IMAGE
1	TIE	23	GNOME	45	ROLL	67	CHALK
2	NOAH	24	NERO	46	ROACH	68	CHEF
3	MU	25	NAIL	47	RAKE	69	SHIP
4	RYE	26	NOTCH	48	ROOF	70	KISS
5	LAW	27	NECK	49	ROPE	71	CAT
6	SHOE	28	KNIFE	50	LACE	72	CANE
7	COW	29	KNOB	51	LOT	73	COMB
8	FEE	30	MOUSE	52	LANE	74	CAR
9	BEE	31	MAT	53	LOOM	75	COAL
10	TOES	32	MOON	54	LURE	76	CASH
11	TOT	33	MUMMY	55	LILY	77	CAKE
12	TIN	34	MOWER	56	LEECH	78	COFFEE
13	TOMB	35	MULE	57	LOCK	79	COP
14	TIRE	36	MATCH	58	LAVA	80	FOZZIE
15	TOWEL	37	MIG	59	LIP	81	FAT
16	DASH	38	MOVIE	60	CHEESE	82	FAN
17	TACK	39	MOP	61	SHEET	83	FOAM
18	DIVE	40	RICE	62	CHAIN	84	FIRE
19	TUB	41	RAT	63	CHIME	85	FILE
20	NOSE	42	RAIN	64	CHERRY	86	FISH
21	NET	43	RAM	65	JAIL	87	FOG
22	NUN	44	ROWER	66	CHOO-CHOO	88	FIFE

89	FIB	102	DASANI (WATER)	115	DOODLE	128	DNF (DID NOT FINISH)
90	BUS	103	TISMA (NICARAGUA)	116	TOT SHOE	129	TOWN B(ALL)
91	BAT	104	TASER	117	DIET C(OKE)	130	TUMS
92	BONE	105	TASSEL	118	TWO DOV(ES)	131	TOMATO
93	BUM	106	TOE SASH	119	TIE TUB(ES)	132	DEMON
94	BEAR	107	TUSK	120	TOONS	133	DAM A M(OAT)
95	BELL	108	TEA SIEVE	121	TNT (DYNAMITE)	134	DIMMER (SWITCH)
96	BEACH	109	TEASPOON	122	TNN (THE NASHVILLE NETWORK)	135	TAMALE
97	BOOK	110	TOOTSIE	123	DENIM	136	DAMAGE
98	PUFF	111	TOOTED	124	TENOR	137	DIM MAK (DEATH TOUCH)
99	PIPE	112	TITAN	125	TUNNEL	138	DMV (DEPARTMENT OF MOTOR VEHICLES)
100	DAISIES	113	TATUM (O'NEAL)	126	DANISH	139	DUMP
101	TEST	114	TATER (TOT)	127	TANK	140	DRESS

141	TREAT	149	TRAP	157	TALC (TALCUM POWDER)	165	DISH L(ADY)
142	TRON	150	TAILS	158	TALL FOE	166	TWO CHOO-CHOO(S)
143	TRAM	151	TILT	159	TULIP	167	TIE CHOK-(ING)
144	TERROR	152	TALON	160	DITCHES	168	TWO SHIV(S)
145	TRAIL	153	TULUM (MEXICO)	161	TIE A SHEET	169	TOSHIBA
146	TRASH	154	TAILOR	162	TOUCH KNEE	0	SAW
147	TRACK	155	TALL EEL	163	DOUCHE ME		
148	DRIV(ER)	156	TOOL CH(EST)	164	TEACHER		

Your goal for this chapter is to know these images so well that, when you see the number, you'll instantly think of the image. When I first started to study them, I went by the thermostat in the house, and it read NUN degrees Celsius. Then I knew, when I saw the number 22 as NUN, I was ready.

After studying this chapter, you should have a good knowledge of each number and the image associated with it.

EXERCISES

Complete the following charts.

86	
90	
137	
168	
88	
132	
140	
49	
6	
96	
24	
45	
39	
116	
156	
70	
3	
22	
83	
69	
91	
13	

TOOTED	
TOMATO	
TATER (TOT)	
RYE	
TOONS	
DOODLE	
FIB	
TRAP	
MOVIE	
DUMP	
CHAIN	
TRASH	
CAKE	
DIET C(OKE)	
LANE	
TAILOR	
PUFF	
TIE TUB(ES)	
TEST	
CASH	
TIE CHOK(ING)	
SHEET	

35			RAKE	
144			CHERRY	
152			FIRE	
169			DASH	
51			DISH L(ADY)	
138			NET	
40			FOZZIE	
104			TUMS	

CHAPTER HARD C OR K

HOLE CARDS HAVE A RICH
HISTORY OF NICKNAMES

In this chapter, we will associate an image with each starting set of hole cards in Texas Hold'em, the most popular poker game being played right now. When I first thought about creating images for these hands, I decided to go with the traditional images that players have made up for years. Interestingly, pro poker players have been creating images for starting hole hands in Texas Hold'em since the game was created. Why? Most likely it was an attempt to remember their cards more easily. What you are doing with this book is taking their baby steps in memorization (written with the greatest of respect) and advancing them to the pro level. In the next few chapters, you might start to see the applications specifically when you have a decision to make at the poker table that could go either way. What I think separates the pros from the amateurs are the tough pots, those in which the call is almost 50/50 and you are barely ahead and scoop the pot. This part of the book will give you a tremendous edge in such situations and a feeling like you are in the major league while everyone around you is still in little league. In fact, Paul, a close friend of mine, when I first showed him just the VPIP part of my techniques, told me, "I have never had such a clear vision of the table, it was almost like they were playing with their cards up, and I knew exactly where I was going to chip up."

Below is a list with an explanation of the hand to help you with the image if need be. Some of the images will be considered derogatory by many; of course, no offense is intended. Most of these names were created by players themselves before political correctness was the norm.

AA	AMERICAN AIRLINES
KK	COWBOYS
QQ	SIEGFRIED AND ROY
JJ	FISH HOOKS
TT	DIMES
99	WAYNE GRETZKY
88	SNOWMEN
77	HOCKEY STICKS
66	ROUTE 66
55	SPEED LIMIT
44	SAILBOATS
33	CRABS
22	DUCKS
AK	BIG SLICK
AQ	BIG CHICK
AJ	BLACKJACK
AT	JOHNNY MOSS (Named for him in his honor)
A9	MIKE MCDERMOT (Hand in the movie *Rounders* he loses his stack with)
A8	DEAD MAN'S HAND (Wild Bill Hickok's hand when he was shot)
A7	SLAPSHOT (Bullet from a hockey stick)
A6	ASICS (This one is mine; I liked the runner better than the other names)
A5	HIGH FIVE
A4	TRANSVESTITE (It looks like Aces, but the second Ace changed into a 4.)
A3	ASHTRAY
A2	HUNTING SEASON (A duck is going to get a bullet in the head.)

KQ	MARRIAGE
KJ	KOJAK
KT	KITE (This one is also mine, easier than the other images.)
K9	CANINE
K8	KATE (King and 8 put together)
K7	KING COBRA (I liked this one better than Kevin, the older image.)
K6	KICKS (King and 6 put together)
K5	KNIVES (King and 5 put together)
K4	FORK (King and 4 put together)
K3	KING CRAB
K2	DONALD DUCK (king of the ducks)
QJ	MAVERICK (from the song in the movie *Queens and Jacks*)
QT	QUENTIN TARANTINO
Q9	QUEEN BEE (This one is also mine; I found it easier to remember B being the ninth sound.)
Q8	KUWAIT
Q7	COMPUTER HAND (Computers decided that this was the absolute average winning hand; in our ranking, suited it is 53rd and unsuited it is 116th in a full table.)
Q6	QUEEN LATIFAH IN BED (This one is also mine; I needed an image I wouldn't easily forget.)
Q5	GRANNY MAY (Queen is the Granny, 5 is for May, the fifth month.)
Q4	HOUSEWORK (What's a queen for?)
Q3	GAY WAITER (a Queen with a tray)
Q2	DAISY DUCK (queen of the ducks)
JT	JUSTIN TIMBERLAKE
J9	T.J. CLOUTIER (Cloutier made three straight flushes with this hand the same year)

J8   JEFFREY DAHMER (He ate Jack.)

J7   JACK DANIELS (Jack Daniels No. 7 whisky)

J6   RAILROAD HAND (sounds like a train going over tracks when you say "Jacks and sixes" really fast, over and over)

J5   JACKSON 5 OR MOTOWN

J4   FLAT TIRE (What's a jack for?)

J3   LUMBERJACK (a Jack and a trey or tree)

J2   HECKLE AND JECKLE (the two jays from Spy vs. Spy)

T9   COUNTDOWN

T8   TETRIS (looks like a Tetris move)

T7   SPLIT OR BOWLING (10–7 split in bowling)

T6   SWEET 16

T5   WOOLWORTH'S (five and dime store)

T4   TRUCKER'S HAND

T3   TYLENOL 3 (This one is mine, found it easier.)

T2   DOYLE BRUNSON (He won two WSOP titles, 1978 and 1979, with this hand.)

98   OLDSMOBILE (The 1989 Oldsmobile was something else.)

97   STU UNGAR (This one is mine; the last time he won the main event and the only true three-time champion of the World Series.)

96   DINNER FOR TWO (sexual position)

95   DOLLY PARTON

94   JOE MONTANA

93   JACK BENNY

92   TWIGGY (29 is the measurement of a flat-chested model.)

87   RPM (When the first record single came out, it spun at 87 RPM.)

86   MAXWELL SMART

85	OCHO CINCO
84	BIG BROTHER
83	REVOLVER
82	TADPOLE (what a duck ate)
76	UNION OIL
75	HEINZ (57 varieties of soup)
74	DOUBLE DOWN (In blackjack, you double down on 74.)
73	DUTCH WAITER (Sven with a tray)
72	WHIP (worst hand in poker)
65	RETIREE
64	BLUE BALLS (What is sex for? This one is mine.)
63	BLOCKY (from Doyle Brunson's Super System)
62	VODKA (26 ounces in a bottle)
54	JESSE JAMES (his Colt .45)
53	BULLY JOHNSON
52	QUARTER
43	BOOK (What's a tree for?)
42	STUD (2 x 4 in building houses)
32	MICHAEL JORDAN

When you know all of these images like the back of your hand, move on. I know it seems as if you are doing a lot of mundane studying right now, but trust me: this is the groundwork for being able to instantly recall information at the table. The better your foundation, the faster and easier information will come to you later. Put the hard work in today for a lifetime of easy poker decisions.

If you didn't know before, now you know all the nicknames for the Texas Hold'em hands.

EXERCISES

Complete the following charts.

76		KING COBRA	
K6		QUEEN LATIFAH IN BED	
QT		COMPUTER	
74		KNIVES	
88		JOHNNY MOSS	
44		HECKLE AND JECKLE	
Q4		SIEGFRIED AND ROY	
97		KATE	
43		HOUSEWORK	
K9		BLOCKY	
AJ		DOLLY PARTON	
73		FISH HOOKS	
T5		KUWAIT	
A2		QUARTER	
JT		MOTOWN	
92		VODKA	
A8		DAISY DUCK	
TT		ROUTE 66	
QJ		SPLIT	
T2		BULLY JOHNSON	

CHAPTER F

THE PEG SYSTEM

Now that you have learned the images for all 169 numbers and the images associated with all the different types of hands, we will use a combination of the peg system for memory (used by Harry Lorayne in *The Memory Book*) and association for memory to enable you to quickly memorize all 169 hands in order of rank. If memorizing all 169 hands in order of rank isn't challenging enough, I found two different ranking systems: one I use for full table play, the other I use for stealing strategies when often I am heads-up. The peg system involves associating your image of the number with the image of the thing you are trying to remember — in this case the image for the hole card — putting them together in a way that you can remember.

Before I learned that memory can be trained, I tried to learn all of the cards in order of rank. I made flash cards and studied pretty hard. After 10 days, I gave up because I always messed up one or two of them and barely learned the top 20. I was trying to learn the old rote way, and it took forever and was extremely tedious. Two years later I found the old cards collecting dust and decided to give it another try, this time after I had learned to train my memory. In less than five minutes, I had memorized the top 30 hands, and it felt effortless. I hadn't even perfected the images I really wanted. After I came up with all my images later, I had them memorized in one hour. You might find that amazing, but what I find even more amazing is that any card player willing to work on his game can do it very easily provided he has his memory trained. If that wasn't enough, I found a different ranking system for heads-up play, which I also memorized quickly and easily once I had my images. Imagine, in less than two hours with this system, you can commit all 169 hole card rankings to memory and know exactly where you sit suited, unsuited, full table, or heads-up. Find me a player who can do that without this system!

Below are the 169 Texas Hold'em hands and their rankings against a full-ring table with images to remember them. This will get you used to picturing the image associated with each set of hole cards. Later I will provide a complete table of all the images I use, and you can associate them however you wish. I will use the full-table rankings throughout the book for examples.

AA	AMERICAN AIRLINES	TIE	an American Airlines flight full of ties
KK	COWBOYS	NOAH	Noah dressed as a cowboy
QQ	SIEGFRIED AND ROY	MU	Siegfried on one end and Roy on the other of the mu symbol
JJ	FISH HOOKS	RYE	fish hooks stuck in a rye bottle
TT	DIMES	COW	cow with dimes for legs
99	WAYNE GRETZKY	DASH	Dash wearing the 99 Oilers jersey
88	SNOWMEN	GNOME	garden gnome between two snowmen
77	HOCKEY STICKS	RICE	hockey sticks made out of rice
66	ROUTE 66	ROOF	roof made out of Route 66 signs
55	SPEED LIMIT	CHAIN	chain sparking down highway at speed limit

44	SAILBOATS	CAT	sails with pictures of cats on them
33	CRABS	FILE	You open a file, and tons of hermit crabs attack you.
22	DUCKS	BAT	bat-eating ducks
AK S/UN	BIG SLICK S/UN	LAW(S)/TOES (UN)	law symbol with toes in the scales covered in a big oil slick
AQ S/UN	BIG CHICK S/UN	SHOE(S)/ TOWEL(UN)	big chick in a towel wearing huge clown shoes
AJ S/UN	BLACKJACK	BEE(S)/ NET(UN)	bees caught in a net playing blackjack to get out
AT S/UN	JOHNNY MOSS	TIN(S)/ MOUSE(UN)	giant tin mouse with the head of Johnny Moss
A9 S/UN	MIKE MCDERMOT	NOSE(S)/ LACE(UN)	Mike has a huge nose with lace coming out.
A8 S/UN	DEAD MAN'S HAND	NAIL(S)/ SHEET(UN)	dead man wrapped in a sheet with a huge nail in his head
A7 S/UN	SLAPSHOT	MAT(S)/ SHIP(UN)	You are shooting pucks on a giant ship sailing on a giant mat.
A6 S/UN	ASICS	MULE(S) FOAM(UN)	foam mule wearing huge, brand-new Asics runners
A5 S/UN	HIGH FIVE	MOON(S)/ CANE(UN)	canes high-fiving each other on the moon
A4 S/UN	TRANS- VESTITE	MOWER(S)/ FOZZIE(UN)	Fozzie Bear dressed in drag mowing your lawn
A3 S/UN	ASHTRAY	MIG(S)/ FIB(UN)	Pinocchio flying a Mig through a bunch of ashtrays
A2 S/UN	HUNTING SEASON	RAT(S)/ TEST(UN)	rat taking a test on hunting rabbits

KQ S/UN	MARRIAGE	FEE(S)/ TUB(UN)	married couple in a tub filled with fees
KJ S/UN	KOJAK	TOT(S)/ NERO(UN)	Nero is a tot with the head of Telly Savalas
KT S/UN	KITE	TIRE(S)/ MUMMY(UN)	mummy flying a tire kite
K9 S/UN	CANINE	NUN(S)/ LEECH(UN)	canine dressed like a nun biting a leech
K8 S/UN	KATE	MOVIE(S)/ FIRE(UN)	Kate Hudson on fire in a movie theater
K7 S/UN	KING COBRA	ROWER(S)/ BOOK(UN)	rower rowing across a sea of books getting away from a king cobra
K6 S/UN	KICKS	RAKE(S)/TOE SASH(UN)	foot kicking a rake has a toe sash
K5 S/UN	KNIVES	ROPE(S)/ TOOTED(UN)	When you pull a rope tied to knives on one end, it toots a horn.
K4 S/UN	FORK	LANE(S)/TIE TUB(ES)(UN)	Forks are tying tubes in a lane of traffic.
K3 S/UN	KING CRAB	LAVA(S)/ TENOR(UN)	lava river full of king crabs and tenors
K2 S/UN	DONALD DUCK	JAIL(S)/ TOMATO(UN)	Donald Duck in a jail packed with tons of tomatoes
QJ S/UN	MAVERICK	TOMB(S)/ KNIFE(UN)	Maverick in King Tut's tomb with a knife stuck in him
QT S/UN	QUENTIN TARANTINO	TACK(S)/ MATCH(UN)	Quentin with a tack for one leg and a match for the other
Q9 S/UN	QUEEN BEE	NOTCH(S)/ CHIME(UN)	queen bee ringing chimes with notches all over them and her

Q8 s/un	KUWAIT	RAIN(s)/ BEAR(un)	oil raining on a bear in Kuwait
Q7 s/un	COMPUTER HAND	LOOM(s)/TOT SHOE(un)	computer at a loom spinning a tot's shoe
Q6 s/un	QUEEN LATIFAH IN BED	CHEESE(s)/ TUNNEL(un)	Queen Latifah having sex with cheese shaped like a tunnel
Q5 s/un	GRANNY MAY	CHALK(s)/ DAM A M(OAT) (un)	Granny May dead on a moat dam with a chalk outline
Q4 s/un	HOUSEWORK	KISS(s)/DIM MAK(un)	KISS doing homework, their boss yells at them, they kill him with the dim mak or death touch
Q3 s/un	GAY WAITER	CAKE(s)/ TREAT(un)	The gay waiter has a cake and tons of treats on his tray.
Q2 s/un	DAISY DUCK	COFFEE(s)/ TRAIL(un)	Daisy Duck is running on a trail made out of coffee beans.
JT s/un	JUSTIN TIMBERLAKE	DIVE(s)/ MOP(un)	Justin dives on a mop, killing himself.
J9 s/un	T.J. CLOUTIER	KNOB(s)/ CHERRY(un)	T.J. has a knob on his forehead and cherries on his chin.
J8 s/un	JEFFREY DAHMER	ROLL(s)/ BONE(un)	Jeffrey Dahmer has a bone and a cinnamon roll for dinner.
J7 s/un	JACK DANIELS	LOCK(s)/DIET C(OKE)(un)	Jack Daniels is locked to a giant can of Diet Coke.
J6 s/un	RAILROAD	CASH(s)/ DRESS(un)	railroad made out of cash and dresses
J5 s/un	JACKSON 5	FAN(s)/ TRON(un)	The Jackson 5 in Tron suits are blown away by a huge fan.

J4 S/UN	FLAT TIRE	FIFE(S)/ TRASH(UN)	flat tires with fifes sticking in them on a pile of trash
J3 S/UN	LUMBERJACK	BELL(S)/ TRAP(UN)	lumberjack caught in a trap ringing a bell for help
J2 S/UN	HECKLE AND JECKLE	DAISIES(S)/ TULUM(UN)	Heckle and Jeckle are stomping on daisies at Tulum ruins in Mexico.
T9 S/UN	COUNT- DOWN	NECK(S)/ LIP(UN)	The neck and lip are voicing out a countdown.
T8 S/UN	TETRIS	RAM(S)/ FISH(UN)	fish with ram's horns playing Tetris
T7 S/UN	SPLIT	LURE(S)/ TATER(UN)	Lures hooked into tater tots bowling just got 10-7 splits.
T6 S/UN	SWEET 16	COAL(S)/ DAMAGE(UN)	A girl for her sweet 16 gets a new car and crashes it into a huge pile of coal.
T5 S/UN	WOOL- WORTH'S	PUFF(S)/ TOLLS(UN)	Puff the Magic Dragon goes into every Woolworth's store and has to pay a toll.
T4 S/UN	TRUCKER	DASANI(S)/ TALON(UN)	truck hauling a huge Dasani water bottle filled with eagle talons
T3 S/UN	TYLENOL 3	TASER(S)/TALL EEL(UN)	You are tasered and stung by a tall eel at the same time, so you need Tylenol 3 for the pain.
T2 S/UN	DOYLE BRUNSON	TEASPOON(S)/ TALL FOE(UN)	Doyle is being beaten up by tall foes with teaspoons.
98 S/UN	OLDSMOBILE	ROACH(S)/ BUS(UN)	A roach is driving a school bus in a giant Oldsmobile.

97 s/un	STU UNGAR	LILY(S)/ TITAN(UN)	Stu has a lily and a kraken (from Clash of the Titans) in his shirt pocket.
96 s/un	DINNER FOR TWO	COMB(S)/ DIMMER(UN)	sexual position on top of a comb with a dimmer switch
95 s/un	DOLLY PARTON	BEACH(S)/ TRACK(UN)	Dolly is running track at the beach
94 s/un	JOE MONTANA	TATUM(S)/ TULIP(UN)	Joe Montana is giving a tulip to Tatum O'Neal.
93 s/un	JACK BENNY	TWO DOV(ES) /TIE A SHEET (UN)	Jack Benny is tying a sheet to two doves and flying away.
92 s/un	TWIGGY	TNT(S)/ TEACHER(UN)	A teacher is blowing up Twiggy with TNT
87 s/un	RPM (RECORDS)	LOT(S)/TEA SIEVE(UN)	parking lot full of records and tea sieves
86 s/un	MAXWELL SMART	CHEF(S)/ DNF(UN)	Maxwell Smart the chef DNF cooking school
85 s/un	OCHO CINCO	FOG(S)/ TRAM(UN)	Ocho Cinco is taking a tram through the fog.
84 s/un	BIG BROTHER	TUSK(S)/TOOL CH(EST)(UN)	Big Brother has an elephant tusk in one hand and a tool chest in the other.
83 s/un	REVOLVER	DANISH(S)/ DISH L(ADY) (UN)	With a revolver, you shoot a dish lady holding a Danish.
82 s/un	TADPOLE	TUMS(S)/TWO SHIV(S)(UN)	A tadpole is eating Tums with two shivs in its body.
76 s/un	UNION OIL	DENIM(S)/ CHOO- CHOO(UN)	A Union Oil sign is smashed through by a denim choo-choo.

75 S/UN	HEINZ	COP(S)/ DUMP(UN)		A cop is dumping Heinz ketchup all over his commanding officer.
74 S/UN	DOUBLE DOWN	TISMA(S)/ TILT(UN)		A person is doubling down with a chip that looks like Tisma, Nicaragua, and a pinball machine on tilt.
73 S/UN	DUTCH WAITER	TOON(S)/ TOUCH KNEE(UN)		A cartoon is touching the Dutch waiter's knee.
72 S/UN	WHIP	TAMALE(S)/ TOSHIBA(UN)		whip whipping a Toshiba TV with tamales pouring out of it
65 S/UN	RETIREE	CAR(S)/ DEMON(UN)		A retiree is in a car with a demon in the passenger seat.
64 S/UN	BLUE BALLS	COMB(S)/ TERROR(UN)		You comb your blue balls in terror.
63 S/UN	BLOCKY	TOOTSIE(S)/ TALC(UN)		a block with tootsie rolls and talcum powder in it
62 S/UN	VODKA	TANK(S)/ TWO CHOO-CHOO(S)(UN)		You fill a tank and two choo-choos with vodka.
54 S/UN	JESSE JAMES	FAT(S)/ DMV(UN)		a fat Jesse James on his driver's license
53 S/UN	BULLY JOHNSON	PIPE(S)/ DRIV(ER)(UN)		What else do bullies need but a pipe and a golf driver to beat you up?
52 S/UN	QUARTER	DOODLE(S)/ DITCHES(UN)		Tons of quarters fill the pockets of a doodler and ditches.
43 S/UN	BOOK	TASSEL(S)/ TAILOR(UN)		a tassel in a book being sewn together by a tailor

42 S/UN	STUD	TNN(S)/ DOUCHE ME(UN)	Picture The Nashville Network with commercials for 2x4s and douches.
32 S/UN	MICHAEL JORDAN	TOWN B(ALL) (S)/TIE CHOK(ING) (UN)	Picture Jordan at a town ball choking everyone with his tie.

Below are the rankings according to actual win rates versus any two random cards against one opponent. As you can see, the rankings are quite different.

HAND	SUITED 9–10 RANK	9–10 RANK	SUITED HU RANK	HU RANK	FULL SUITED IMAGES	FULL UNSUITED IMAGES	HU IMAGES
AA		1		1		TIE	TIE
KK		2		2		NOAH	NOAH
QQ		3		3		MU	MU
JJ		4		4		RYE	RYE
TT		7		5		COW	LOO
99		16		6		DASH	SHEA (STADIUM)
88		23		7		GNOME	KEY
77		40		9		RICE	BAY
66		48		17		ROOF	TOQUE
55		62		27		CHAIN	NOOK (ELEC-TRONIC READER)
44		71		48		CAT	REF

33		85		66		FILE	CHEECH (AND CHONG)
22		91		87		BAT	FIG
AK	5	10	8	12	LAW	TOES	FUTON
AQ	6	15	10	14	SHOE	TOWEL	TOASTER
AJ	9	21	11	15	BEE	NET	TOAD DUEL
AT	12	30	13	19	TIN	MOUSE	DIMETAPP
A9	20	50	18	25	NOSE	LACE	DEVON-LEIGH
A8	25	61	21	32	NAIL	SHEET	ANT MINE
A7	31	69	24	36	MAT	SHIP	NAIR M*A*S*H
A6	35	83	31	41	MULE	FOAM	MEAT ROT
A5	32	72	30	40	MOON	CANE	MACE ROSE
A4	34	80	35	49	MOWER	FOZZIE	MALL RUPI
A3	37	89	37	53	MIG	FIB	MIG LAMB
A2	41	101	46	59	RAT	TEST	RASH LUBE
KQ	8	19	16	23	FEE	TUB	DOJO NEMO
KJ	11	24	20	26	TOT	NERO	NOOSE NASH
KT	14	33	22	33	TIRE	MUMMY	NANNY MUMMY
K9	22	56	29	39	NUN	LEECH	NIP MAP
K8	38	84	43	51	MOVIE	FIRE	ROOM LIGHT
K7	44	97	44	58	ROWER	BOOK	ROWER LEAF
K6	47	106	50	62	RAKE	TOE SASH	LICE CHIN

K5	49	III	54	69	ROPE	TOOTED	LAIR SHOP
K4	52	II9	60	74	LANE	TIE TUB(ES)	CHESS CURRY
K3	58	I24	63	80	LAVA	TENOR	SHAMMY (SHAMOIS) FACE
K2	65	I3I	71	86	JAIL	TOMATO	KITT FUDGE
QJ	13	28	28	38	TOMB	KNIFE	NEWFIE MOVING
QT	I7	36	34	47	TACK	MATCH	MARE WRECK
Q9	26	63	42	56	NOTCH	CHIME	RUIN LATCH
Q8	42	94	52	68	RAIN	BEAR	LOON SHAVE
Q7	53	II6	61	77	LOOM	TOT SHOE	CHAT QUACK
Q6	60	I25	67	81	CHEESE	TUNNEL	CHUCK FEET
Q5	67	I33	72	89	CHALK	DAM A M(OAT)	CONE VIBE
Q4	70	I37	76	93	KISS	DIM MAK	CATCH PASS
Q3	77	I4I	82	98	CAKE	TREAT	VAN ABOVE
Q2	78	I45	88	I05	COFFEE	TRAIL	FIVE DIESEL
JT	18	39	45	57	DIVE	MOP	REEL LUCKY
J9	29	64	55	70	KNOB	CHERRY	LILACS
J8	45	92	65	79	ROLL	BONE	CHILI CUP
J7	57	II7	75	92	LOCK	DIET C(OKE)	CLIPON (TIE)
J6	76	I40	85	I02	CASH	DRESS	FLOATS ON

J5	82	142	91	107	FAN	TRON	BYTE DISK
J4	88	146	95	111	FIFE	TRASH	PLEATED TEA
J3	95	149	97	116	BELL	TRAP	BAKED TUSH
J2	100	153	104	122	DAISIES	TULUM	DESERT NINE
T9	27	59	64	78	NECK	LIP	CHAIR CAVE
T8	43	86	73	91	RAM	FISH	CAM IPOD
T7	54	114	84	101	LURE	TATER	FAIRY DUST
T6	75	136	96	112	COAL	DAMAGE	PATCHED DANE
T5	98	150	106	123	PUFF	TAILS	TOYS SHOOTIN' 'EM
T4	102	152	108	126	DASANI	TALON	OATS FATTEN SHUE (ELIZABETH SHUE)
T3	104	155	114	131	TASER	TALL EEL	TUTOR DOMED
T2	109	158	118	135	TEASPOON	TALL FOE	TODD EVADE MOLLY
98	46	90	83	99	ROACH	BUS	FAME BABY
97	55	112	94	109	LILY	TITAN	BART SPY
96	73	134	103	120	COMB	DIMMER	TEES MIT-TENS
95	96	147	113	121	BEACH	TRACK	TOTEM TENT

94	113	159	124	140	TATUM	TULIP	TONER TREES
93	118	161	127	144	TWO DOV(ES)	TIE A SHEET	TUNIC DRIER
92	121	164	132	149	TNT	TEACHER	DEMAND RUB
87	51	108	100	117	LOT	TEA SIEVE	DISEASED DUKE
86	68	128	110	128	CHEF	DNF	DETEST NAVY
85	87	143	119	137	FOG	TRAM	TEE TOP TEE MUG
84	107	156	130	148	TUSK	TOOL CH(EST)	TEAM STRIVE
83	126	165	139	157	DANISH	DISH L(ADY)	DUMP IT LAKE
82	130	168	142	159	TUMS	TWO SHIV(S)	TURNTABLE
76	66	123	115	133	CHOO-CHOO	DENIM	TATTLE TO MOM
75	79	139	125	141	COP	DUMP	TEEN LITTERED
74	103	151	134	151	TISMA	TILT	TIMER TILT
73	120	162	143	160	TOONS	TOUCH KNEE	DRUM DISHES
72	135	169	152	165	TAMALE	TOSHIBA	TALENT GEL
65	74	132	129	145	CAR	DEMON	TAN PETROL
64	93	144	138	154	BUM	TERROR	DUMB FIDDLER

63	110	157	147	162	TOOTSIE	TALC	TRICKED GIN
62	127	166	156	167	TANK	TWO CHOO-CHOO(S)	TOOLSHED CHICK
54	81	138	136	153	FAT	DMV	DAMAGED LIME
53	99	148	146	161	PIPE	DRIV(ER)	TORCHED CHUTE
52	115	160	155	166	DOODLE	DITCHES	DELI LUDE CHOCHY
43	105	154	150	164	TASSEL	TAILOR	TILE STASHER
42	122	163	158	168	TNN	DOUCHE ME	TY LOVED CHEVY
32	129	167	163	169	TOWN B(ALL)	TIE CHOK(ING)	DESHAM-MIED SHIP

I have put the images together so that, when you first get a hand in poker, you can quickly deduce which image you need — whether it is suited or not. The next step is to memorize each set of hole cards on its own with its own image. Eventually, you will look at your hole cards and remember just the one image you need: J4 unsuited is trash, and Q3 suited is cake. It shouldn't take you longer than an hour or two to commit them to memory with the images I have provided. Then practice them until you know each image without thinking about it. Each image and number should roll off your tongue quickly and easily.

For the second set of images, I might have combined certain numbers. For example, TOASTER, DEVONLEIGH, and PATCHED DANE when sounded out are numbered 1014, 1825, and 96112 respectively. Obviously, no card is ranked 961, so you have to split them in your head to represent 96th and 112th along with 10th and 14th and 18th and 25th. We used other images to cut down on confusion so you don't remember several images that are the same for each set of hole cards.

You now know all 169 images in order of rank for full-table and heads-up play. Weeks of study have been cut down to mere hours, and you will be able to apply what you have learned in many ways in the coming chapters.

EXERCISES

Use your newly memorized images and rank the different sets of hole cards by a numbered rank for each one.

	RANK 9–10	RANK HU
76s		
K6		
QT		
74s		
88		
44		
Q4s		
97		
43		
K9s		
AJ		
73s		
T5s		
A2		
JTs		
92s		
A8		

TT		
QJ		
T2s		
K7s		
Q6		
Q7s		
K5s		
AT		
J2		
QQ		
K8		
Q4		
63s		
95s		
JJ		
Q8		
52		
J5s		
62s		
Q2		
66		
T7		
53s		

CHAPTER B

VPIP: YOUR GATEWAY TO
PRO DECISION MAKING

In this chapter, we will build a foundation for knowing exactly how many hands a player has played. I first used this information in an online program called Poker Tracker. In fact, when I was first searching for a way to connect memory techniques to poker, VPIP was my "eureka" moment. I knew it was likely that no one had thought of bringing the statistics of the online world to a live game mainly because it was thought to be impossible to mentally keep track of all the information a poker tracker can track. For those of you unfamiliar with VPIP, it is an acronym for how often a player *v*oluntarily *p*uts money *i*nto a *p*ot. The key word here is *voluntarily*. If a player does not *voluntarily* put the money into the pot, it does not count. For example, if the player is in the big blind and checks, because she doesn't voluntarily put money into the pot, it does not count towards her VPIP and therefore her hand count does not go up. If she is in the small blind and she completes the call due to pot odds, that does count because she *voluntarily* put money in. If she raises in the BB position when she could have checked, then she does voluntarily put money into the pot, and that will raise her hand count. VPIP is widely used in multi-tabling in the online world. It instantly gives the player a sense of exactly how tightly or loosely an opponent has been playing and therefore an understanding of their hand range. This in turn helps determine how strong or weak a player's hand is in relation to their opponent's.

For example, did you know the exact math on a hand such as AT, which from the previous chapter we know is ranked 30th, has a 54% chance of winning against any two random hole cards a player has inside a VPIP range of 20% or six of his last 30 hands? Now let's increase the player's VPIP — let's say he plays 60% or 18 of his last 30. What is your probability now? Well, you increased it from just a few percentage points over a coin flip to a 61% chance of winning the hand on any of his random two cards within that 60% hand range. You can use this methodology in your decision-making process for the tougher situations you might find yourself in. It also immediately gives you a range of hands far more accurate than you are likely accustomed. In short, as your players' activity rises, so does the strength of all hands you may have seen as marginal. As your opponents tighten up, the values of these same marginal hands decrease significantly.

You can likely see now the endless possibilities of your highly developed memory at the table. My goal is to turn you into a virtual computer at the table with a vast database of information that sinks into your long-term memory. My hope is that, if you play against me, you take it easy on me and conveniently forget what I am doing! Imagine the power you are now playing with. Most of the population can remember seven things for 30 seconds — that's it. *Seven things for 30 seconds!* You are already on your way to zapping tons of information into your brain at a rate far faster than the vast majority of the population.

In order to give you an idea of how easy it is to keep track, I want to provide an example with one player at the table. Let's call her Leissa, after my wife, and let's put her in seat 10. The first step in determining VPIP is to pay attention to where the dealer button is on the table and associate that player as the first player, where the first hand is played. Let's assume his name is Juan, and let's put Juan in seat 1, or the small blind. I now want you to go back in your mind to Chapter L where we created items in your room for the LOCI method. For this exercise, we only need the first two rooms with 10 items. Do you have those 10 items in your mind's eye? Good. Now every time Leissa plays a hand, I want you to use your destruction or mutilation technique to destroy the items in sequence. If you were to use my house as an example, I would destroy my couch first, then my coffee table and so on every time she played a hand. We are at the table and we shall go through two revolutions. Each time Leissa plays a hand, I want you to destroy the next item in your house file in order.

HAND 1	FOLDS
HAND 2	CALLS
HAND 3	RAISES
HAND 4	FOLDS
HAND 5	FOLDS
HAND 6	FOLDS
HAND 7	CALLS
HAND 8	(IN BIG BLIND) CHECKS
HAND 9	(IN SMALL BLIND) COMPLETES (CALLS)
HAND 10	RAISES
HAND 11	FOLDS
HAND 12	FOLDS
HAND 13	RAISES
HAND 14	FOLDS
HAND 15	FOLDS
HAND 16	FOLDS
HAND 17	FOLDS
HAND 18	(IN BIG BLIND) RAISES
HAND 19	(IN SMALL BLIND) FOLDS
HAND 20	FOLDS

Now if you have done this correctly, you will have destroyed seven items in order. I destroyed everything up to and including the stove in my kitchen. This is how to keep track of VPIP for one player. Keeping track of 10 players is the same, only you have different items for each player you are destroying. Leissa has played seven out of 20 hands; if you divide by two and multiply by 10, you will get the percentage of VPIP she has played. In this particular situation, seven divided by two is 3.5, 3.5 times 10 is 35%. Another way to do it (which you will learn later in the chapter) is 1/20 is 5%, five times seven is 35%.

So what does 35% of hands mean? Well, later in the book, I will show you how to easily memorize accurate hand ranges, but in short Leissa is playing AA–66, any suited ace, any suited KQJT98 above 7, and any unsuited AKQJT above 9. Those are approximately the top 35% of the 169 hands. As you can see a wide variety of hands fit into this range.

This is a small example of how you will be using the system on a larger scale. If you can do this easily, keeping track of 10 players is no different. You will easily remember with a little practice what files you have destroyed for each person. The next step is to get started on our numerous files for each opponent at the table. The person after the dealer will always have the images of your first set regardless of the movement of the dealer button. Just like in the example with Leissa, every time she plays a hand you destroy the next image in her set of images. The key is to get at least 25 to 30 images in each set that are completely different. The first experiment I did was to use numbers for all positions, and I quickly wound up becoming confused. Once I separated each seat, with its own set of images or places I had created, it became easy to discern the last thing that player did and record it mentally.

The lists below are my sets of images I use to keep track of a full table. Each seat has its own set of 30 plus images. I would advise you just memorize just two to three sets for two to three players at the table at first. As you become fluent with those, memorize another three sets and then finally four more sets to give you a complete arsenal of images to track the table. Remember memorizing this many images seems daunting, but they are all in order and these should make sense to you. If you don't like some of my sets, memorize easier sets for yourself. Just make sure they are different and you have about 30 of them.

Dealer Number	Images
SEAT 1	alphabet images
SEAT 2	object images
SEAT 3	house (upper floor)

SEAT 4				house (lower floor)
SEAT 5				office images
SEAT 6				Oscar Best Picture winners 1931 to 1960
SEAT 7				United States
SEAT 8				Super Bowl winners
SEAT 9				the human body
SEAT 10				Oscar Best Picture winners 1961 to 1990

When I started my memory training, I memorized a lot of information that isn't used everyday. I think it is pretty cool knowing that the 30th state in alphabetical order is New Jersey. I will give you a list of all the images I use for each seat and how I use them.

ALPHABET IMAGES

For each letter, picture the image and run through them all a few times. Shouldn't take more than five times and you will have them. The importance of remembering these images in order is less than when you did it for the card sequences. All you have to do is move from A to B to C and destroy each image one by one in sequence. You won't have to quickly recall that the letter N is number 14, only that you destroyed the image for letter N (NET). I have also associated my number images with them so you can easily tell in your mind which number is associated with which letter.

A	APPLE	1	TIE	a tie worming through an apple
B	BALL	2	NOAH	Noah with a ball for a head
C	CAMP	3	MU	campfire in the shape of a MU
D	DIRT	4	RYE	bottle of rye full of dirt
E	ELEPHANT	5	LAW	an elephant as a lawyer

F	FOX	6	SHOE	a fox that lives in a shoe
G	GHOST	7	COW	a ghostly cow
H	HOUSE	8	FEE	tons of fees as a roof on the house
I	IGUANA	9	BEE	an iguana with a bee's yellow and black stripes
J	JESTER	10	TOES	a jester with *huge* toes for facial features
K	KNIGHT	11	TOT	a toddler in a suit of armor
L	LOON	12	TIN	a loon made out of tin
M	MITTEN	13	TOMB	a tomb with a mitten over it
N	NOOSE	14	TIRE	a noose tied to a tire from a tree limb
O	OTTER	15	TOWEL	an otter drying off with a huge towel
P	PIE	16	DASH	Dash running through a pie
Q	QUILT	17	TACK	millions of tacks in a quilt
R	RAVINE	18	DIVE	dive into the Grand Canyon ravine
S	STAR	19	TUB	a star in your tub
T	TAPE	20	NOSE	a broken nose taped up
U	UMBRELLA	21	NET	a leaky umbrella made out of a net
V	VINE	22	NUN	a nun with vines growing out of her limbs
W	WEDDING	23	GNOME	a wedding of garden gnomes
X	X-RAY	24	NERO	the skeleton of Captain Nero in an x-ray
Y	YANKEE	25	NAIL	Babe Ruth's bat shaped like a giant nail

Z	ZEBRA	26	NOTCH	a zebra with a huge notch taken out of it
AA	AMERICAN AIRLINES	27	NECK	a plane with a neck before the cockpit
AB	ABDOM-INAL MUSCLE	28	KNIFE	ab muscle with a knife in it
AC	AIR CONDI-TIONING	29	KNOB	an air conditioner with a giant knob
AD	ADVER-TISEMENT	30	MOUSE	Mickey Mouse ad for *Fantasia*

OBJECT IMAGES

1	ROCKET	A rocket looks like a big number 1.
2	SWAN	The number 2 looks like a swan.
3	PYRAMID	There are three pyramids in Egypt made of triangles.
4	FANTASTIC FOUR	Marvel Comics' superhero team.
5	STAR	A star has five points.
6	COLT	The Colt was a six-shooter.
7	CRAPS	lucky seven in craps
8	SNOWMAN	The number 8 looks like a snowman.
9	GORDIE HOWE	Gordie's number
10	FINGERS	You have 10 fingers.
11	REMEMBRANCE DAY	On the 11th hour of the 11th day of the 11th month, World War I ended.

12	DIRTY DOZEN	the movie
13	BAKER	a baker's dozen
14	VACATION	a two-week vacation
15	TENNIS	first point in tennis
16	LICENSE	when many can drive
17	HARRY POTTER	when a wizard becomes an adult
18	ADULT	when you can serve in the army
19	JOHNNY UNITAS	Johnny's number
20	DARTBOARD	the top number in a dartboard
21	COLLEGE DRUNK	legal drinking age
22	RIFLE	a small-powered rifle (.22 caliber)
23	MICHAEL JORDAN	Michael's number
24	BEER	Beer comes in 24 bottles a case.
25	SILVER	a silver anniversary
26	VODKA	comes in 26 ounces
27	PERFECT RUBIK'S CUBE	3x3x3 is 27 or a perfect cube.
28	HORMONES	A woman's special time is every 28 days.
29	LEAP YEAR	February has 29 days in a leap year.
30	MONTH	the number of days in a month

HOUSE FILES (UPPER AND LOWER) AND OFFICE IMAGES

House files I would like *you* to create. Imagine you have two floors in your house. I have five rooms, and I go through them clockwise. I also have five different sections of my basement in which I put things in order clockwise.

You can use the house files you created in Chapter L here, but you'll need to create another set for the next seat. If you do not have a lower floor, you can use any area you know in your surroundings. Keep in mind you need 25 to 30 images in your area in clockwise order. For my office images I started in my parkade and created all of the things I saw until I got to my office. Of course I took the scenic route, but it still worked. You can also create a set of 25 office images or any walk in your mind. The important thing is to have the images so you can quickly destroy them in your head and keep track of the VPIP. Create them for seats three, four, and five.

OSCAR BEST PICTURE WINNERS

You will be using these images for seats six and ten. In seat six you will use best pictures from 1931 to 1960, and you can use images from 1961 to 1990 for seat ten. For this set, I associate each movie with the image of the last two numbers of the year: that is, the first Academy Awards ceremony crowned the first best picture for 1928 or 28 or knife. Our knife has a set of wings and flies away, so our first best picture was *Wings*. For later exercises, I start my count with 1931 so it is easier to keep track of which number the person played — the best picture that year was *Cimarron*. Also, you will not need all of the images provided for this one, but I thought that, if you are going to memorize 60 of them, you might as well memorize all of them and amaze your friends. Having said that, if you would rather save time and get to the end of the chapter, memorize 60 and move on, but I highly recommend that you memorize them all to give your memory a good workout.

1928	WINGS	KNIFE	a knife with wings flying away
1929	A BROADWAY MELODY	KNOB	a knob featuring a Broadway show
1930	ALL QUIET ON THE WESTERN FRONT	MOUSE	Mickey Mouse on the Western Front
1931	CIMARRON	MAT	a mat with a simulated AARON on it

♥
♣
♦

1932	THE GRAND HOTEL	MOON	a grand hotel on the moon
1933	CAVALCADE	MUMMY	a cavalcade of mummies
1934	IT HAPPENED ONE NIGHT	MOWER	a mower mowing pens at night
1935	MUTINY ON THE BOUNTY	MULE	a mule on the ship *The Bounty*
1936	THE GREAT ZIEGFELD	MATCH	a match lighting a big zig-zag felt
1937	THE LIFE OF ÉMILE ZOLA	MIG	a Mig shooting at a Life cereal box with Émile Zola inside
1938	YOU CAN'T TAKE IT WITH YOU	MOVIE	a movie screening of a funeral
1939	GONE WITH THE WIND	MOP	a mop blown away in tornado-force winds
1940	REBECCA	RICE	a girl you knew named Rebecca made out of rice
1941	HOW GREEN WAS MY VALLEY	RAT	a rat racing up and down a green valley
1942	MRS. MINIVER	RAIN	It's raining minivans.
1943	CASABLANCA	RAM	A ram rams through Rick's Café Americain.
1944	GOING MY WAY	ROWER	A rower asks you if you are "going my way."
1945	THE LOST WEEKEND	ROLL	A roll goes into a time machine and skips over a weekend, losing it.
1946	THE BEST YEARS OF OUR LIVES	ROACH	a roach having the best time of his life

1947	GENTLEMAN'S AGREEMENT	RAKE	a rake combing a gentleman's hair
1948	HAMLET	ROOF	a roof made out of skulls
1949	ALL THE KING'S MEN	ROPE	"all the king's men" hanging from a noose
1950	ALL ABOUT EVE	LACE	Eve (from Adam and Eve) wearing lace
1951	AN AMERICAN IN PARIS	LOT	Paris in a parking lot with a cowboy in the middle
1952	THE GREATEST SHOW ON EARTH	LANE	A circus is in your lane.
1953	FROM HERE TO ETERNITY	LOOM	a loom made out of a bottle of Eternity cologne
1954	ON THE WATERFRONT	LURE	A lure is cast on the waterfront.
1955	MARTY	LILY	Marty has a lily face and body.
1956	AROUND THE WORLD IN 80 DAYS	LEECH	a leech in a balloon circling the world
1957	THE BRIDGE ON THE RIVER KWAI	LOCK	a lock through the middle of the bridge
1958	GIGI	LAVA	a lava flow of GIGIs coming at you
1959	BEN-HUR	LIP	Charlton Heston with *huge* lips
1960	THE APARTMENT	CHEESE	a huge apartment made out of cheese
1961	WEST SIDE STORY	SHEET	a huge sheet going down the west side of a building

1962	LAWRENCE OF ARABIA	CHAIN	Lawrence chained to the Arabian desert
1963	TOM JONES	CHIME	Tom Jones chiming a song
1964	MY FAIR LADY	CHERRY	Instead of swallowing a marble, "my fair lady" swallows a cherry.
1965	THE SOUND OF MUSIC	JAIL	the sound of music in prison
1966	A MAN FOR ALL SEASONS	CHOO-CHOO	A man is on a train with four cars: one is summer, one is winter, one is fall, and one is spring.
1967	IN THE HEAT OF THE NIGHT	CHALK	A chalk line is around a body on a really hot night.
1968	OLIVER	CHEF	The chef is frying up Oliver.
1969	MIDNIGHT COWBOY	SHIP	The ship has a cowboy on it, and it's midnight.
1970	PATTON	KISS	General Patton is shooting at KISS.
1971	THE FRENCH CONNECTION	CAT	A cat is in a French outfit with a beret.
1972	THE GOD-FATHER	CANE	The Godfather has a cane.
1973	THE STING	COMB	A comb is run through Sting's hair.
1974	THE GOD-FATHER PART 2	CAR	The Godfather driving a huge Ferrari
1975	ONE FLEW OVER THE CUCKOO'S NEST	COAL	coal billowing out of a cuckoo's nest

1976	ROCKY	CASH	Rocky Balboa swimming in cash in the ring
1977	ANNIE HALL	CAKE	Annie Hall jumping out of a cake
1978	THE DEER HUNTER	COFFEE	a deer hunter jumping in a giant cup of coffee
1979	KRAMER VS. KRAMER	COP	a cop in court with both Kramers
1980	ORDINARY PEOPLE	FOZZIE	Fozzie Bear being punched by ordinary people
1981	CHARIOTS OF FIRE	FAT	fat chariots on fire
1982	GANDHI	FAN	Gandhi being blown away by a giant fan
1983	TERMS OF ENDEARMENT	FOAM	terms and conditions being written on a giant foam mattress
1984	AMADEUS	FIRE	Mozart's hair on fire
1985	OUT OF AFRICA	FILE	a file shaped like Africa
1986	PLATOON	FISH	Charlie Sheen looks like a fish in Vietnam.
1987	THE LAST EMPEROR	FOG	Out of the fog comes a great emperor.
1988	RAIN MAN	FIFE	Dustin Hoffman playing the fife
1989	DRIVING MISS DAISY	FIB	Pinocchio driving the car
1990	DANCES WITH WOLVES	BUS	Kevin Costner driving a bus through a tipi
1991	SILENCE OF THE LAMBS	BAT	A bat swoops down and eats all the lambs.

1992	UNFORGIVEN	BONE	You get shot in the Wild West in your femur.
1993	SCHINDLER'S LIST	BUM	a big list of shins on a bum
1994	FORREST GUMP	BEAR	a grizzly bear chasing Forrest Gump
1995	BRAVEHEART	BELL	Mel Gibson as Braveheart banging a huge bell
1996	THE ENGLISH PATIENT	BEACH	a patient being treated on a beach
1997	TITANIC	BOOK	a book with four smokestacks sinking
1998	SHAKESPEARE IN LOVE	PUFF	Puff the Magic Dragon as Shakespeare
1999	AMERICAN BEAUTY	PIPE	a tobacco pipe with an American flag and a beautiful girl on it
2000	GLADIATOR	SAW	gladiators fighting with saws
2001	A BEAUTIFUL MIND	TIE	a tie around a beautiful brain
2002	CHICAGO	NOAH	Noah singing and dancing in Chicago
2003	LORD OF THE RINGS: RETURN OF THE KING	MU	rings being thrown around the MU symbol
2004	MILLION DOLLAR BABY	RYE	a baby drinking rye on top of a million dollar stack of money
2005	CRASH	LAW	a car crashing into a law symbol
2006	THE DEPARTED	SHOE	a shoe departing on a plane
2007	NO COUNTRY FOR OLD MEN	COW	a cow in the country being kicked by old men

2008	SLUMDOG MILLIONAIRE	FEE	Millionaire dogs in slums have a lot of fees.
2009	THE HURT LOCKER	BEE	a bee hurt in a locker
2010	THE KING'S SPEECH	TOES	toes coming out of the king's mouth while he makes a speech

UNITED STATES

Again for this set memorizing all 50 states isn't necessary; memorize 30 and move on if need be. Yet again I encourage you to memorize all of them to get your brain working and to become used to memorizing quickly with this method.

ALABAMA	TIE	an album wearing a tie
ALASKA	NOAH	Noah freezing in Alaska
ARIZONA	MU	a MU flying through the Arizona desert
ARKANSAS	RYE	an ark filled with rye whiskey
CALIFORNIA	LAW	a law symbol filled with cauliflower
COLORADO	SHOE	a shoe filled with the Rocky Mountains
CONNECTICUT	COW	a cow as a doctor connecting a cut
DELAWARE	FEE	a fee in a big Tupperware dish
FLORIDA	BEE	a bee stuck in an orange
GEORGIA	TOES	George Foreman with monster toes
HAWAII	TOT	a tot in Hawaii saying aloha
IDAHO	TIN	a tin Idaho potato
ILLINOIS	TOMB	You are ill in a tomb.

INDIANA	TIRE	A tire rolls over an Indian.
IOWA	TOWEL	a towel soaked in iodine
KANSAS	DASH	Dash plays for the Kansas City Chiefs
KENTUCKY	TACK	a tack going through Kentucky Fried Chicken
LOUISIANA	DIVE	Louise from *The Jeffersons* diving into a pool
MAINE	TUB	a tub racing down Main Street
MARYLAND	NOSE	a giant nose marrying a piece of land
MASSACHUSETTS	NET	Boston Bruins' net
MICHIGAN	NUN	a nun with an itchy gun
MINNESOTA	GNOME	A gnome plays for the Minnesota North Stars.
MISSISSIPPI	NERO	Nero on a Mississippi riverboat
MISSOURI	NAIL	A nail in your head causes misery.
MONTANA	NOTCH	a notch out of a mountain
NEBRASKA	NECK	a neck with new brass Ks stuck in it
NEVADA	KNIFE	a giant knife stuck in the middle of the Vegas Strip
NEW HAMPSHIRE	KNOB	A knob is stuck on your new hamper.
NEW JERSEY	MOUSE	Mickey Mouse plays for the Devils.
NEW MEXICO	MAT	a mat of the Mexican flag
NEW YORK	MOON	The Empire State Building is now on the moon.
NORTH CAROLINA	MUMMY	a mummy facing north and caroling

NORTH DAKOTA	MOWER	a mower facing north cutting down the Native leader Dakota
OHIO	MULE	a mule bucking a really high O
OKLAHOMA	MATCH	Oklahoma City lit up by a match
OREGON	MIG	a Mig with a giant ore gun shooting ore
PENNSYLVANIA	MOVIE	a movie about the Pittsburgh Steelers
RHODE ISLAND	MOP	an island riding a mop
SOUTH CAROLINA	RICE	rice facing south and caroling
SOUTH DAKOTA	RAT	a rat chewing on Dakota facing south
TENNESSEE	RAIN	It is raining on 10 Nessies.
TEXAS	RAM	a ram charging into the Alamo
UTAH	ROWER	a rower rowing across a salt lake
VERMONT	ROLL	Bob Newhart eating a ton of rolls
VIRGINIA	ROACH	a roach with the Virgin Mary for a face
WASHINGTON	RAKE	George Washington raking leaves
WEST VIRGINIA	ROOF	Virgin Mary on the roof of a house in the Wild West
WISCONSIN	ROPE	a rope made out of cheese
WYOMING	LACE	lace wrapped around a wired mink

SUPER BOWL WINNERS

This one is neat, though there are some back-to-back winners that can confuse you. The first two winners, for example, are the Green Bay Packers. So, for the first one, I use an image of Vince Lombardi, and for the second one I use Bart

Starr. Memorizing the winners of each Super Bowl is pretty cool too. Just like in the previous examples, associate each image number with the team. This time I want you to come up with your own associations for practice.

TIE	GREEN BAY PACKERS
NOAH	GREEN BAY PACKERS
MU	NEW YORK JETS
RYE	KANSAS CITY CHIEFS
LAW	BALTIMORE COLTS
SHOE	DALLAS COWBOYS
COW	MIAMI DOLPHINS
FEE	MIAMI DOLPHINS
BEE	PITTSBURGH STEELERS
TOES	PITTSBURGH STEELERS
TOT	OAKLAND RAIDERS
TIN	DALLAS COWBOYS
TOMB	PITTSBURGH STEELERS
TIRE	PITTSBURGH STEELERS
TOWEL	OAKLAND RAIDERS
DASH	SAN FRANCISCO 49ERS
TACK	WASHINGTON REDSKINS
DIVE	LOS ANGELES RAIDERS
TUB	SAN FRANCISCO 49ERS
NOSE	CHICAGO BEARS
NET	NEW YORK GIANTS
NUN	WASHINGTON REDSKINS
GNOME	SAN FRANCISCO 49ERS
NERO	SAN FRANCISCO 49ERS
NAIL	NEW YORK GIANTS
NOTCH	WASHINGTON REDSKINS
NECK	DALLAS COWBOYS
KNIFE	DALLAS COWBOYS
KNOB	SAN FRANCISCO 49ERS
MOUSE	DALLAS COWBOYS

MAT	GREEN BAY PACKERS
MOON	DENVER BRONCOS
MUMMY	DENVER BRONCOS
MOWER	ST. LOUIS RAMS
MULE	BALTIMORE RAVENS
MATCH	NEW ENGLAND PATRIOTS
MIG	TAMPA BUCANEERS
MOVIE	NEW ENGLAND PATRIOTS
MOP	NEW ENGLAND PATRIOTS
RICE	PITTSBURGH STEELERS
RAT	INDIANAPOLIS COLTS
RAIN	NEW YORK GIANTS
RAM	PITTSBURGH STEELERS
ROWER	NEW ORLEANS SAINTS
ROLL	GREEN BAY PACKERS

THE HUMAN BODY

These are pretty neat areas in which to store information. When doing your counts, you can destroy different body parts on your opponent. They are all in order with the first side (I use the left side) as muscular and the right side as skeletal.

TOP OF THE HEAD
EYES
NOSE
MOUTH
CHIN
SHOULDER
BICEPS
TRICEPS
FOREARM
HAND
HIP

QUADRICEPS

HAMSTRING

CALF

FOOT

TOE

TIBIA

FIBULA

FEMUR

PELVIS

FINGER

RADIUS

ULNA

HUMERUS

CLAVICLE

Now that you have the images associated with each person sitting at the table, the counts can begin. First I find where the dealer button is in accordance with the actual dealer on the table. Then I count how many hands inclusive will be played to the dealer (assuming no one gets knocked out) and put my number image on him. So, if it is six hands inclusive to the dealer, I imagine him sitting in a big shoe; then, when it passes him, I add six or nine or whatever seats are in the game.

As the players play, I use the destruction method to determine which image they are on. For example, the first hand starts on seat two. Seats five and six fold, and seat seven raises to 200. I now destroy the first image associated with seat seven. In this case, it is the great state of Alabama. I picture a nuclear explosion destroying the entire state. Seat eight calls. Now I picture Vince Lombardi exploding. Seat nine folds, seat one folds. I now have my first set of counts. I do this for each hand and then do the math when the hand count reaches 10. At this point, I get a sense of how active a player is. I pay particular attention to anyone who has played six or seven hands out of 10 and who has played one hand. Both players are exploitable. Hopefully, you have the looser players to your right and the tighter ones to your left. I then continue my counts until the dealer has dealt 30 hands or until a break happens, at which point, if you have taken statistics, you know that 30 points of data become statistically relevant. A player's habits no doubt become illuminated right in front of your eyes. I reset after each break to see if any players have thought about their play and are changing their game.

Times to start your counts over are immediately after a loose player gets cracked for a big pot, after every two hours in a major tournament, after a break or if you see a player start to get frustrated with her lack of hands. I have noticed major gear shifts in all of these scenarios. For instance, in my league at home, a player sat down and literally played 80% of his hands over the first 10 hands, and my mental database recorded hands as weak as 10-4 offsuit played in position five. When he raised on the button, I looked down at an AT suited and calculated that I was probably ahead of any two random hole cards in that range. In fact, my odds of winning the hand based on this particular opponent's hand range were exactly 64%. I reraised, he shoved, I snap called. He flipped over AK, which I wasn't exactly happy to see, but you can understand my reasoning behind the call. I caught a 10 on the river and stacked him for almost all of his chips. He asked me how I could call, and I told him he had played 80% of his hands and how I had genuinely thought it was an easy call. I was fortunate to catch a 10, but after that hand I recounted his activity for the next 10 hands. He played one hand! In fact, he raised that hand, and I had AJ offsuit, which I folded at that point knowing full well he likely had me beat. This was all within about a 45-minute time frame. Using this methodology, I was able to shift gears along with my opponents, and I wound up winning that tournament. Yes, I got lucky with the 10, but with this system you don't have to get lucky as often, and you'll wind up making far better decisions.

The whole point of VPIP counts is to be able to shift gears along with your opponents and play hands optimally against them and exploit how tight or loose they are. It also gives you the bonus of hiding how tight or loose you are because your play can now depend on how each opponent plays at the table, giving you a true random activity for each hand played, further mixing up your play. For example, a loose aggressive player raises from mid-position and has played 75% of his hands, and you pick up AJ suited. You will learn later that you have at least a 60% win rate against any two random cards your opponent might have. Behind you left to act are two players who have been fairly tight, 15% and 20%. You know that by reraising you are likely not getting shoved by the two tight players unless they have AA, KK, or some other monster. You also know that, if you are called by Mister Loose Aggressive, you can feel free to pound the flop turn and river knowing that you likely have them beat depending, of course, on flop texture and other factors.

Now let's look at the next hand, where a tight player raises and you have AQ suited. You will learn later that you need the player to be playing at least 25% of her hands to be a 60% favorite on any two random cards she has. This particular player is at 10%; that limits you to AA, KK, and QQ for a shove. You also look behind you, and you have two relatively short stacked loose cannons who call almost with any two cards. You can elect to fold the AQ suited in light of your situation at that point and wait for a better spot. Notice that this is a stronger hand than the last hand but plays weaker because of who is involved in the pot based solely on VPIP.

Using this information in this manner will enable you to make excellent pre-flop decisions based on stats taken from the game live: statistics that no one else will have on you or on anyone else. They will be blind, but you shall see. Only through techniques of memorization can you contain the wealth of statistical information at the table. You will also notice your stack volatility go down and your decision-making ability go up.

You have now learned that each seat has a list of about 25 to 30 images for you to destroy in order to have an accurate VPIP on your opponents. This goes a long way toward deducing a range for your opponent and knowledge for you to exploit it.

MAKING EASY CALCULATIONS AT THE TABLE

Below I have inserted a table of the exact percentages of one hand out of one (100%) to one hand out of 30 (3.33%). Memorizing this list will make it very easy for you to calculate in your head a quick percentage of VPIP.

Hands	%
1	100%
2	50%
3	33%
4	25%
5	20%
6	17%
7	14%
8	13%
9	11%

10	10%
11	9%
12	8%
13	8%
14	7%
15	7%
16	6%
17	6%
18	6%
19	5%
20	5%
21	5%
22	5%
23	4%
24	4%
25	4%
26	4%
27	4%
28	4%
29	3%
30	3%

Now you will notice that a lot of the later numbers have the same percentages, so for ease we can group those numbers and simplify the chart:

12, 13	8	TIN TOMB	FEE

14, 15	7	TIRE TOWEL	COW
16–18	6	DASH DIVE	SHOE
19–22	5	TUB NUN	LAW
23–28	4	GNOME KNIFE	RYE
29, 30	3	KNOB MOUSE	MU

In your mind associate the images and you will have a quick reference guide for each percentage.

Now let's tackle 1–11. Well, the first five are very easy. You do not have to be a math genius to figure out the first five, but in the interest of being complete we shall go through them.

$$1/1 = 100\%$$

$$1/2 = 50\%$$

$$1/3 = 33.33\%$$

$$1/4 = 25\%$$

$$1/5 = 20\%$$

Now this leaves us with four more to remember: 6,7,8, and 9.

$$1/6 = 17\%$$

$$1/7 = 14\%$$

$$1/8 = 13\%$$

$$1/9 = 11\%$$

We can create a story for 6, 7, 8, and 9. There was a giant tack (17) that popped a tire (14) inside the tomb (13) of King Tut (11). So for 6, 7, 8, 9 if you can remember that a giant tack popped a tire in the tomb of King Tut, you will always remember the four percentages you need.

1/10 = 10%

And 1/11 = 9%

Note: you can also remember 1/9 and 1/11 very easily. 1/9 is 11 percent and 1/11 is 9 percent. I call these the emergency numbers 9-1-1.

So now that we have all of our numbers, it's time to come up with examples. The following chart depicts what you may see at a poker table after, say, 14 hands.

Seat	VPIP	Total
1	4	14
2	6	14
3	8	14
4	2	14
5	3	14
6	7	14
7	3	14
8	3	14
9	4	14
10	1	14

Let us quickly deduce what the actual percentages are. Let's start with 14. We know that 14 is tire, and tire and towel are associated with cow, which is 7%. Now it becomes easy, assuming you know your times tables for 7 as a multiplier. Seat one is 7% times 4 = 28%, seat 2 is 7% times 6 = 42%, seat 3 is 7% times 8 = 56%, seat 4 is 7% times 2 = 14%, seat 5 is 7%

times 3 = 21%, seat 6 is 7% times 7 = 49%, seat 7 is 7% times 3 = 21%, seat 8 is 7% times 3 = 21%, seat 9 is 36%, and seat 10 is 7%.

If you want to save an even *further* step you can simply reduce your multiplier as the dealer deals, but this is only an *expert* level counter who could pull this off. Instead of actually counting the hands from the dealer, you could start at 100% being the first hand, and then move to 50%, and then 33.33%, and so on as the dealer deals and just have your multiplier from the dealer instantly. For example, the first hand dealt would be 100; two would be 50; 3, 33.3; 4, 25; 5, 20; 6, 17; and so on. Then multiply it with the player's VPIP. This again would only be used if you were completely fluent in VPIP counts, but it would be very fast and accurate.

Doing the math part of these charts in a live game will quickly and accurately deduce anyone's VPIP into a number you can use to make better decisions. Learning the math is crucial, so make sure you know these tables inside and out.

EXERCISES

Follow the action in the table below and keep an accurate VPIP on each opponent.

Button	Seat	Action
B	1	F
SB	2	F
BB	3	F
	4	F
	5	F
	6	R
	7	C
	8	F
	9	F
	1	F
B	2	F
SB	3	F
BB	4	C
	5	R
	6	C
	7	C
	8	RR
	9	F

	I	R
	2	C
B	3	C
SB	4	F
BB	5	F
	6	F
	7	C
	8	C
	9	C
	I	C
	2	F
	3	F
B	4	R
SB	5	C
BB	6	C
	7	F
	8	F
	9	C
	I	F
	2	F
	3	F
	4	C
B	5	C

SB	6	C
BB	7	C
	8	F
	9	F
	1	C
	2	F
	3	F
	4	F
	5	F
B	6	F
SB	7	F
BB	8	C
	9	R
	1	F
	2	F
	3	F
	4	F
	5	R
	6	C
B	7	F
SB	8	F
BB	9	C

BB	1	F
	2	F
	3	F
	4	F
	5	F
	6	R
	7	C
B	8	RR
SB	9	C
SB	1	F
BB	2	F
	3	F
	4	F
	5	R
	6	RR
	7	C
	8	C
B	9	C
B	1	C
SB	2	C
BB	3	C
	4	F
	5	F

	6	F
	7	F
	8	F
	9	R

Seat	VPIP (%)
1	
2	
3	
4	
5	
6	
7	
8	
9	

CHAPTER TS

A DATABASE COMPUTERS
WOULD DROOL OVER

Building a database on your opponents is an excellent way of deducing their hole cards. In this chapter, we will examine how to remember not only which cards your opponents are playing but also which positions they were in when they played them. You can do this for as few or as many opponents as you wish. In my opinion, the absolute master of this talent is pro poker player Phil Hellmuth Jr. He can remember years later the exact position and raise you made with which hand. I remember in one tournament against T.J. Cloutier that Phil recalled exactly what T.J. had done when he bluffed two years earlier. T.J. did the same thing, and Phil caught him in a bluff. T.J. slowly rolled over his cards and said, "You got me." The dealer pointed out that T.J. misread his hand and had a straight, beating Phil. Although T.J. won the hand, he actually thought he missed and telegraphed that to Phil, and Phil saw it and called. He was correct in seeing the bluff, but after T.J. misread his hand Phil was visibly upset, of course. He said he had waited two years to finally catch T.J. in that bluff, and when he finally did T.J. misread his hand. Phil says he deduces exact hole cards from watching players' exposed hole cards and recalling exactly what they do when they bluff or are strong. He can do this only through acute observation and instant recall of his opponents' actions. That is why he has won 11 wsop bracelets.

This system was my first experiment in memory training, applied to

♥

♣

♦

poker in my league in Winnipeg. I created images for each position at the table. My first images were of hijackers and different guns to represent the different UTG positions and the hijack seat, as well as the cut-off and two blind men for the blinds. I eventually went with countries and cities because doing so enabled me to create more vivid and different images. I also memorized them starting with position three, which is UTG, so I could rapidly stick any exposed hole cards into their slots for players. I found that I got confused after a while with the different countries with different players.

In the end, I decided to create 10 different positions for each player and systematically file each image that represented a set of hole cards to a particular position that would be a unique image for each player. This system would cut down any confusion and enable me to keep a massive amount of easily attainable information.

For each image associated with each player, I find 10 spots in order in which I can place images of hole cards for easy recall. They are as follows:

Position 1	TRAIN
Position 2	NET (GOALIE)
Position 3	MANSION
Position 4	ROLLER COASTER
Position 5	LEXUS
Position 6	SHARK
Position 7	CHRISTMAS TREE
Position 8	FOOTBALL FIELD
Position 9	BEATLES
Position 10	SOLAR SYSTEM

Let's take the first image you will be using if it were a live game of poker. Seat 10 would be the dealer, seat 1 the small blind, and seat 2 the big blind. So we would start off with our first image actually being seat 3, mansion. We need 10 parts of the mansion (one for each position at the table) for us to "place" the images of cards for easier recall. The parts also have to be in order for us to easily remember them. For instance, at the mansion, we could start by driving up the large driveway. That will be the first item representing the first position of seat three. Next could be a garage, then the front door. Then the big staircase and the dining room and so forth until you have 10 places. Try to visualize yourself walking through this opulent mansion filled with expensive items of furniture. The better you visualize yourself walking through it, the better you will remember it.

Below I have itemized all 10 places I use for each image to store images of cards.

	1	2	3	4	5
	Train	Net (Goalie)	Mansion	Roller Coaster	Lexus
1	RAILGUARD	LEFT LEG PAD	DRIVEWAY	LINEUP	BUMPER
2	SMOKEBOX	GLOVE	GARAGE	TICKET PERSON	HEADLIGHTS
3	LIGHT	JERSEY	FRONT DOOR	CAR	HOOD
4	SMOKE-STACK	MASK	STAIRWAY	CLIMB	WIND-SHIELD
5	BELL	BLOCKER	DINING ROOM	DIVE	ROOF
6	CAB	STICK	LIVING ROOM	LOOP	HATCH
7	COAL	RIGHT LEG PAD	KITCHEN	TWIST	TAIL LIGHTS
8	TENDER	GOALPOST	BACK DOOR	SPLASH	REAR BUMPER
9	WHEEL	NET	POOL	PLATFORM	EXHAUST PIPE
10	RAIL	GOAL LIGHT	BACKYARD	EXIT	WHEELS

	6	7	8	9	10
	Shark	**Christmas Tree**	**Football Field**	**Beatles**	**Solar System**
1	SNOUT	STAR	PARKING LOT	JOHN	SUN
2	NOSTRIL	LIGHTS	ENTRANCE	PAUL	MERCURY
3	EYES	BALLS	CONCES-SIONS	GEORGE	VENUS
4	MOUTH	TINSEL	HALLWAY	RINGO	EARTH
5	TEETH	BRANCH	STEPS	MICRO-PHONES	MARS
6	GILLS	TRUNK	SEATS	GUITARS	ASTEROID BELT
7	PECTORAL FIN	GIFTS	PLAYERS	DRUM SET	JUPITER
8	STOMACH	TREE SKIRT	CHEER-LEADERS	STAGE	SATURN
9	DORSAL FIN	TREE HOLDER	GOALPOSTS	AUDIENCE	URANUS
10	TAIL FIN	WATER CUP	ENDZONE	STADIUM	NEPTUNE

You'll notice that all of the images start with the corresponding letter or sound attached to the number. Each time a player shows down a hand, I make a mental image of the hole cards he had and what position they were in and store the image accordingly in that space. Let's say that the player in seat five showed a hand and that he played J4 offsuit in position seven. We would simply imagine trash and lots of it (as the J4 offsuit image is trash) coming out of the tail lights of the Lexus, which represents seat five. Now we can also store another image in the same place. Imagine that the player played AJ offsuit, for which our image is a net. Well, now imagine a net full of trash hooked onto the tail lights. You have now associated the images in that position and not confused it with any other position at the table.

Originally, I used countries for positions for each player but found I confused them, so I had to create a special spot for each image. For some silly reason, I was under the impression that there were many more show-downs in my poker league than there actually were. I was surprised to see many opponents muck their hands and not show. In fact, by the end of the night, I hadn't built up much of a database, but it was enough to get some solid tells and tendencies out of certain active players. This first exercise enabled me to place second that night (I would have placed first had I not been three-outed twice in a row heads-up), and I started to see valuable information that I had never seen with such detail before. I was able to pick up on a great player in our league, Marc Virgo, and how he played his hand. He actually had the best hand, but played the hand very timidly. This allowed me to semi-bluff him off a hand two hands later with the confidence that he would fold. He would never have folded two years ear-lier when he was more confident in his play. I still vividly remember Sean Brooks in Fiji (in my old country system, Fiji was position eight and Poland position nine) raising with KQ offsuit (both red) and Marc smooth-calling with AQ (again both red) in Poland. He check-called Brooks to the river, so I had to comment, "What the hell is wrong with you, Virgo? Why you playing so scared?" To which he replied, "Have you seen what has happened to me the last year and a half?" That to me was an open invitation to raise him out of every pot in which I thought he was weak. Now, Virgo actually won that pot, with top-pair Queens and top kicker, but that night he had it in his head that he was going to be outdrawn in every hand. I would not have noticed had I not been focusing on trying to build a database on my opponents.

In league or home game play, this is especially powerful because your database will only grow with each passing game. Then you can instantly recall that Marc Virgo, for example, has played bee, toes, tin, towel, law, and tub in the mansion pool. He plays hands as weak as cherry, trash, neck, bone, and bus in the mansion dining room. This is what a powerful memory can do for you — you can associate all of those images and run through them instantly while playing a hand. Eventually, most if not all poker players are prone to patterns. Some are not. Fortunately, you'll get chips from the many who have patterns.

Now, if the hand was raised, you can color the image of the cards red, blue if the player limped, and yellow if she called a raise. Doing so will help you to understand what the player could be raising or limping with in later hands.

An alternative method for remembering the hands is to use the players themselves to store the information. Start at the head of the player and go clockwise to the shoulder, hand, knee, foot, ankle, shin, forearm, elbow, and chin. Number them one through 10 respectively, and physically put the image in the position on their bodies. Then all you have to do is visualize where the images are and you will have a database in your mind of the hands they play.

Your exercise for this chapter is to log on to an online poker website and start with five-minute sessions at tables with nine players. Poker Stars allows you to review the hands played should you keep the table open. Memorize as many exposed cards as possible and whether or not the hand was raised or limped pre-flop. Build a mental database on each player in each position at online speed. Later write down each player, his hands, and how he played them in each position. Then go back and review each hand. Once you have each player's hand perfect, increase your session and repeat the process. After you master a session, build up the next one by five minutes. If you can keep track at online speeds, you will have no trouble keeping track at live games since online games are approximately two to three times faster. Your goal is to build a perfect database of hands for each player after a one-hour session of watching an online table. You want to maximize your ability to create and store many different images without thinking for instant recall later. When you have mastered this skill, move on to the next chapter.

You have now learned how to build a database of hole cards on your opponents that will help you to make tighter decisions like the pros do. Hopefully, by mastering this chapter, you'll be able to catalog every hand an opponent plays against you and play her tendencies better and nail down the cards she played.

EXERCISES

Look at the following table. Your goal is to memorize the hand counts, the hole cards played in each position, and whether the player raised, limped, or called a raise with those cards.

Button	Seat	Pre-Flop	SHDWN
B	I	F	
SB	2	F	
BB	3	F	
	4	F	
	5	F	
	6	F	
	7	R	AKS
	8	C	AQ
	9	C	77
	I	F	
B	2	F	
SB	3	F	
BB	4	F	
	5	F	
	6	R/C	JTS
	7	R	KQ
	8	F	
	9	F	

♥

♣

♦

	I	F	
	2	F	
B	3	C	89
SB	4	C	55
BB	5	C	A2
	6	R	ATS
	7	F	
	8	F	
	9	F	
	I	F	
	2	F	
	3	R	A9S
B	4	F	
SB	5	C	J9
BB	6	C	54
	7	F	
	8	F	
	9	F	
	I	R	QQ
	2	F	
	3	F	
	4	C	T9S
B	5	C	AQ

SB	6	F	
BB	7	C	AA
	8	F	
	9	F	
	1	F	
	2	F	
	3	F	
	4	F	
	5	F	
B	6	R	J8s
SB	7	F	
BB	8	C	A4
	9	F	
	1	F	
	2	F	
	3	F	
	4	R	88
	5	C	KTs
	6	C	QJ
B	7	F	
SB	8	F	
BB	9	F	

BB	I	C	T2S
	2	F	
	3	F	
	4	F	
	5	F	
	6	F	
	7	F	
B	8	F	
SB	9	R	84
SB	I	C	34
BB	2	C	86s
	3	F	
	4	F	
	5	R	AK
	6	F	
	7	F	
	8	F	
B	9	C	JJ
B	I	C	74S
SB	2	C	AJS
BB	3	C	Q4
	4	F	
	5	F	

	6	F	
	7	F	
	8	F	
	9	R	TT

CHAPTER TT

HAND RANGES TO

INCREASE YOUR ODDS

In this chapter, we will memorize each percentage of hands played and the associated number of hands in that range. For example, five percent has eight hands, 10% has 17 hands, and so on. We will also easily memorize hand ranges from five percent of hands played to 80% of hands played; although they won't be exact (if you are a perfectionist, you can), I will give you a close range for each set of pairs, suited cards, and non-suited cards. This will help you to easily determine the strength of your hand ranking versus the number of hands your opponent has played or to further eliminate certain hands that an opponent could have when combining it with the VPIP learned in the previous chapter. If you are an avid poker player and have some semblance of betting patterns, you can have an amazing ability to nail down the two hole cards a person has. Every 10% is 16.9 hands or approximately 17 hands. We will round up or down, whichever is closer to each level.

First off will be the number of hands for each percentage. I have changed some of the images so that you won't become confused with earlier training and so that, if the same number comes up twice in the series, you won't use the same image twice. The image will still be derived from the same rules we used for the number images we used in the past. After you have learned the percentages, I will show you how I use them to determine the relative strength of my hand versus my opponent's range.

Percentage	# of Hands	Images	
5	8	LAW	IVY
10	17	TOES	TICK
15	25	TOWEL	NILE
20	34	NOSE	MIR
25	42	NAIL	RUN
30	51	MOUSE	LIGHT
35	59	MULE	LOBE
40	68	RICE	CHIVE
45	76	ROLL	CAGE
50	85	LACE	FOWL
55	93	LILY	BOOM
60	101	CHEESE	TOAST
65	110	JAIL	DADDIES
70	118	KISS	TIE DIVE
75	127	COAL	DONK
80	135	FOZZIE	TWO MOLE(S)
85	144	FILE	TERRIER
90	152	BUS	TOW LINE
95	161	BELL	TOUCHED

Now we will learn the system for hand ranges. When I first started to come up with the system, I wanted to be as exact as possible and memorize each set of cards. The only issue was that there was a lot to remember, and it was pretty complicated if you were sitting at the table. A friend said I had to make it easier, so that is exactly what I did. Below, you will see the actual tables of the hand ranges (they are for full-table play), and I have taken the complexity out.

Note that some traditional sound images for this chapter have been changed to make life easier. T will represent 10, Q will represent a *K* sound, Jack a *J* sound. I found the system easier to do this way. Less work and quicker thoughts at the table are obviously better than more work and slower thoughts.

Let's examine how to use the image and what you will be thinking about at the poker table. The top five percent is right below. You'll notice that the image is TEAK since it is wood for a table. It is short for TQ. The first letter is a 10, and that means this range plays all pairs — Aces through 10s. The next letter is for suited cards; in this case, it's a Q for Queen. This means that any suited cards above Queen are in the range. AK, AQ, and KQ are in. QJ is not because the Jack is lower than the bar that is the Queen. Two letters, one image, and you have your range.

Top 5%	8 hands	
Images	TQ	**TEAK**
Pairs	AA–TT	
Suited AX	AKS–AQS	
Suited KX	KQS	

Top 10%	17 hands	
Images	9	TQ	**BOUTIQUE**
Pairs	AA–99	
Suited AX	AKS–ATS	
Suited KX	KQS–KTS	
Suited QX	QJS–QTS	
AX	AK–AQ	

Now let's go on to a more complicated one, top 15% or FOOTAGE. You'll notice in this range that the F represents an 8 for pairs, so that is your pair range — Aces through 8s, but you'll notice that the next one is T for 10 and that suited Aces go down to A8s and suited Kings go down to K9s. But the rest are down to a 10 (QTs and JTs), so I rounded up. You will miss out on three hands, but to make it easier we will just remember the 10, which I am sure you will agree with. The next image in FOOTAGE ends with a J sound and represents J for Jack. So, for unsuited cards, the lowest card will be a Jack. AK, AQ, AJ, KQ, KJ, and QJ. Three cards for pairs suited and unsuited.

Top 15%	25 hands		
Images	8 T J		FOOTAGE
Pairs	AA—88		
Suited AX	AKS—A8S		
Suited KX	KQS—K9S		
Suited QX	QJS—QTS		
Suited JX	JTS		
AX	AK—AJ		
KX	KQ—KJ		

Now let's go to 25% of hands. In this one, you'll notice that the image is COOKING BAIT. Hard C is 7, so pairs AA—77. The next one is KING; well, it represents King. I put it in so you know that you now start at the King because any suited Ace is in this range. So the next range is KING B or King, and the lowest card is now 9. So it's any suited Ace, KQ—K9, QJ—Q9, JT—J9, and T9. T represents 10 and the end, so unsuited cards are any card above a 10.

Top 20%	34 hands		
Images	8 9 J		V BADGE
Pairs	AA—88		
Suited AX	AKS—A4S		
Suited KX	KQS—K9S		
Suited QX	QJS—Q9S		

Suited JX	JTS–J9S
Suited TX	T9S
AX	AK–AT
KX	KQ–KT
QX	QJ

Top 25%	42 hands		
Images	7 K9 T	**COOKING**	
		BAIT	
Pairs	AA–77		
Suited AX	Any suited Ace		
Suited KX	KQS–K8S		
Suited QX	QJS–Q8S		
Suited JX	JTS–J9S		
Suited TX	T9S		
AX	AK–AT		
KX	KQ–KT		
QX	QJ–QT		
JX	JT		

Top 30%	51 hands		
Images	6 K8 T	**CHECKING**	
		FOOT	
Pairs	AA–66		
Suited AX	Any suited Ace		

Suited KX	KQS–K5S
Suited QX	QJS–Q8S
Suited JX	JTS–J8S
Suited TX	T9S–T8S
Suited 9X	98S
Suited 8X	87S
AX	AK–A9
KX	KQ–KT
QX	QJ–QT
JX	JT

Top 35%	59 hands
Images	CHOKING COP
Pairs	AA–66
Suited AX	Any suited Ace
Suited KX	KQS–K3S
Suited QX	QJS–Q7S
Suited JX	JTS–J7S
Suited TX	T9S–T7S
Suited 9X	98S–97S
Suited 8X	87S
AX	AK–A9
KX	KQ–K9
QX	QJ–QT
JX	JT

TX	T9

Top 40%	68 hands
Images	LOW QUEEN CAB
Pairs	AA–55
Suited AX	Any suited Ace
Suited KX	Any suited King
Suited QX	QJs–Q5s
Suited JX	JTs–J7s
Suited TX	T9s–T7s
Suited 9X	98s–97s
Suited 8X	87s–86s
Suited 7X	76s
AX	AK–A8
KX	KQ–K9
QX	QJ–Q9
JX	JT–J9
TX	T9

Top 45%	76 hands
Images	ROW QUEEN CHUBBY
Pairs	AA–44
Suited AX	Any suited Ace
Suited KX	Any suited King
Suited QX	QJs–Q4s

Suited JX	JTS–J6S
Suited TX	T9S–T6S
Suited 9X	98S–96S
Suited 8X	87S–86S
Suited 7X	76S
Suited 6X	65S
AX	AK–A5
KX	KQ–K9
QX	QJ–Q9
JX	JT–J9
TX	T9

Top 50%	85 hands
Images	**MY JACK SHIP**
Pairs	AA–33
Suited AX	Any suited Ace
Suited KX	Any suited King
Suited QX	Any Queen suited
Suited JX	JTS–J5S
Suited TX	T9S–T6S
Suited 9X	98S–96S
Suited 8X	87S–86S
Suited 7X	76S–75S
Suited 6X	65S
Suited 5X	54S

AX	AK–A4
KX	KQ–K8
QX	QJ–Q9
JX	JT–J9
TX	T9

Top 55%	93 hands
Images	A JACK LOAF (A for *any*)
Pairs	Any pair
Suited AX	Any suited Ace
Suited KX	Any suited King
Suited QX	Any Queen suited
Suited JX	JTS–J4S
Suited TX	T9S–T6S
Suited 9X	98s–96s
Suited 8X	87s–85s
Suited 7X	76s–75s
Suited 6X	65s–64s
Suited 5X	54s
AX	AK–A3
KX	KQ–K8
QX	QJ–Q9
JX	JT–J8
TX	T9–T8
9X	98

Top 60%	101 hands
Images	A TEN (DOLLAR) LOCKING FEE
Pairs	Any pair
Suited AX	Any suited Ace
Suited KX	Any suited King
Suited QX	Any Queen suited
Suited JX	Any Jack suited
Suited TX	T9s–T5s
Suited 9X	98s–95s
Suited 8X	87s–85s
Suited 7X	76s–75s
Suited 6X	65s–64s
Suited 5X	54s–53s
AX	Any Ace
KX	KQ–K7
QX	QJ–Q8
JX	JT–J8
TX	T9–T8
9X	98

Top 65%	110 hands
Images	A NINER KING FOE (Dallas Cowboys)
Pairs	Any pair

Suited AX	Any Ace suited
Suited KX	Any King suited
Suited QX	Any Queen suited
Suited JX	Any Jack suited
Suited TX	Any 10 suited
Suited 9X	98s–95s
Suited 8X	87s–84s
Suited 7X	76s–74s
Suited 6X	65s–63s
Suited 5X	54s–53s
AX	Any Ace
KX	KQ–K6
QX	QJ–Q8
JX	JT–J8
TX	T9–T8
9X	98
8X	87

Top 70%	118 hands
Images	A NINE RAKING COW(S)
Pairs	Any pair
Suited AX	Any suited Ace
Suited KX	Any suited King
Suited QX	Any Queen suited
Suited JX	Any Jack suited

Suited TX	Any 10 suited
Suited 9x	98s–93s
Suited 8x	87s–84s
Suited 7x	76s–74s
Suited 6x	65s–63s
Suited 5x	Any 5 suited
AX	Any Ace
KX	KQ–K5
QX	QJ–Q7
JX	JT–J7
TX	T9–T7
9X	98–97
8X	87

Top 75%	127 hands
Images	A(N) EIGHT MAKING CUE(S)
Pairs	Any pair
Suited AX	Any suited Ace
Suited KX	Any suited King
Suited QX	Any Queen suited
Suited JX	Any Jack suited
Suited TX	Any 10 suited
Suited 9x	Any 9 suited
Suited 8x	87s–83s
Suited 7x	76s–73s

Suited 6x	Any 6 suited
Suited 5x	Any 5 suited
AX	Any Ace
KX	KQ–K4
QX	QJ–Q6
JX	JT–J7
TX	T9–T7
9X	98–97
8X	87
7X	76

Top 80%	135 hands
Images	AA QUEEN CHIA
Pairs	Any pair
Suited	Any suited cards
AX	Any Ace
KX	Any King
QX	QJ–Q5
JX	JT–J7
TX	T9–T7
9X	98–96
8X	87–86
7X	76

Here is your completed memorization list with the percentage, number of hands, and range images for hands.

119

♥

♣

♦

Percentage	# of Hands	Images		
5	8	LAW	IVY	TEAK
10	17	TOES	TICK	BOUTIQUE
15	25	TOWEL	NILE	FOOTAGE
20	34	NOSE	MIR	V BADGE
25	42	NAIL	RUN	COOKING BAIT
30	51	MOUSE	LIGHT	CHECKING FOOT
35	59	MULE	LOBE	CHOKING COP
40	68	RICE	CHIVE	LOW QUEEN CAB
45	76	ROLL	CAGE	ROW QUEEN CHUBBY
50	85	LACE	FOWL	MY JACK SHIP
55	93	LILY	BOOM	A JACK LOAF
60	101	CHEESE	TOAST	A TEN (DOLLAR) LOCKING FEE
65	110	JAIL	DADDIES	A NINER KING FOE
70	118	KISS	TIE DIVE	A NINE RAKING COW(S)
75	127	COAL	DONK	A(N) EIGHT MAKING CUE(S)
80	135	FOZZIE	TWO MOLE(S)	AA QUEEN CHIA

Obviously, the later hand ranges might not help you in deducing hole cards for an opponent who is loose. Yet, when a player who is loose appears at the table, you don't have to be an expert to know that, if you pick up a hand as low as T9 suited and are in position, you will get a ton of chips from that person. The only issue is if another player beats you to the punch and empties the stack you want before you get to it. Any time I see a player as loose as 60% or more, I target that player and usually pound him hard pre-flop. I try to get him committed before the flop with marginal hands, knowing that I am likely ahead with a semi-strong to strong hand.

The art of poker comes in when you have a player playing 10% to 30% of her hands. With her range lower, and with a detailed database, you can rest assured you'll be able to put it all together and quickly know which cards she probably has and whether you even want to participate in the hand.

Here is an example. You are in a major tournament in the WSOP. You have been largely card dead for the opening hour, but it doesn't really bother you because you have been making your counts and are very focused on the activity at the table. A few hands have been shown down, so you have built up a small database on a couple of players. You have counted 39 hands and are on your 40th hand and calculating the activity.

Seat 1	ELEPHANT	12.5%	No data
Seat 2	SNOWMAN	Exactly 20%	No data
Seat 3	COMPUTER TABLE	Exactly 30%	A BIG TIN FOR A FRONT DOOR
Seat 4	SOMBRERO	Exactly 25%	No data
Seat 5	PARKADE ELEVATOR	5%	No data
Seat 6	ON THE WATER-FRONT	60%	CHEF AND TEST ON DORSAL FIN KNOB IN GILLS
Seat 7 (you)	ALASKA	5%	
Seat 8	BALTIMORE COLTS	12.5%	No data
Seat 9	TRICEPS	20%	No data
Seat 10	SOUND OF MUSIC	12.5%	LAWYER ON VENUS

♥

♣

♦

The dealer button is on seat 10. Seats one to five fold. Seat six raises the standard 3x raise. His chips have dwindled down to about 2,000, and he has made it 300 to go. You pick up tin, (ATS) position seven. We know from observation of our wild card player that his range is 60%, which enables any pair, any suited Ace, King, Queen, or Jack. Any suited cards higher than 5, with the exception of 6xs and 5xs, which are lower still, any Ace, and about any two cards higher than an 8 unsuited. You will learn in later chapters that your win percentage against any two random cards with ATS is about 60% plus against a player playing 60% of his hands. We also know the hand he played in the SHARK'S GILLS or position six was KNOB or J9 suited. You believe that he is an average player who has been paying some attention to you and knows you are fairly tight, but he really doesn't care much about that since he has played fairly wildly and has not been afraid to put chips in the middle on marginal hands. To your left, you have some fairly experienced tight players who have been watching and know you to have been fairly quiet. The pot is 450 with the blinds. Your stack is at 4,300.

In this situation, with a hand like this, ATS moves from being a marginal hand to a premium hand. I would be very comfortable putting in a big raise against my loose opponent and putting him to a decision for all his chips. If he goes all in (which I doubt he would), then given the information I have I'd feel very comfortable calling him.

So let's put in a raise to, say, 850 total. It is folded around to our loose player, and he calls. He has 1,100 in chips left. The flop comes down 2s 4H 7D. He thinks for a minute and shoves all in. Given what we know about his hand range, it's highly unlikely that he hit any of this flop. He also has employed a stop-and-go move, which is usually designed to get a player to fold. Even though you have complete air here, you might consider a call. There is now 2,900 in the pot and 1,100 left to call, giving you well over a 2:1 call with two overcards if he spiked a 7, which you doubt anyway. Couple that with the fact you would have been happy to go all in against him with this hand in the first place and you call.

He flips over T9 suited, a complete bluff, and you hit an Ace on the turn, ending his tournament.

This is just a detailed look at how you can use the vast amount of information at a live game to make even more powerful decisions. Let's review. You now know exactly how many hands each percentage of cards has, a close estimation of which cards fit in a full-table hand range with that percentage, and how to use this information.

EXERCISES

For each percentage, write down the image associated with the number of cards and the corresponding image for the hand range; then derive the number of cards and the hand range. For example,

55%   LILY   BOOM   A JACK LOAF   Any pair, any suited AKQ,
                                            suited J to 5, and any
                                            unsuited 8 or higher

Now you complete the following:

%	% Image	# Image	Range Image	#	Pairs	Suited	Unsuited
20							
40							
35							
80							
10							

CHAPTER TN

WIN RATES AND HAND RANGES
TO CRUSH YOUR OPPONENTS

In this chapter, we will memorize the complete odds of any two of your known hole cards versus any two random hole cards a player might have against you. We will also look at how strong those hole cards are against varying types of players and how we can memorize optimum hand ranges that will give you a winning edge versus loose or tight players and what your minimum hands should be. I have found this to be extremely useful in almost any stealing situation that a player could be shoving all in with as well as using the knowledge to have an optimum stealing strategy to stay alive in tournaments.

Sometimes in a tournament I have almost no information to go on, and all I have is how active the player is. In fact, in 2006 I was fortunate to make it to the end of day four in the main event, and I had the great misfortune of trying to play against one of the finest professional poker players I have ever played against — Jeffrey Lisandro. To give you an idea of how great he really was, he showed down only a few hands, but each time I was dying to know what he actually had. He varied his raises and almost never played the same hand the same way twice. You had no clue where you stood, and if he caught the slightest hint you were weak he'd shove you and put you to the test. If you ever run into a player like Lisandro, this chapter will be invaluable for you. That is why I put so much emphasis on remembering the VPIP in earlier chapters. When that happens, I let the math do the

♥

♣

♦

talking and make my decision from there. When I first started to use this technique, I was surprised at how accurate it really was. Of course, there will always be players who wake up with monsters, but most of the time the math will guide you to the correct decision. Again, for a complete record, I have included the easy hands such as Aces. I mean, you don't have to be a Phil Ivey to figure out if you should call an all-in before the flop with Aces or Kings, but I thought you'd like to have complete odds.

You will likely find it far more useful with hands such as A9 and A8 or mid-pairs such as 99, 88, 77. Knowing the math before you call an all-in might give you up to a 15% extra edge in the hand: the difference between making a great call or a great lay down, allowing you either to chip up or to save chips — both of which are earned chips getting you closer to a tournament win.

Let's start off by memorizing the complete odds of any two hole cards versus any two random cards. This comes up in tournament situations all the time. However, imagine that you *know* your odds versus any two random cards before you make the call. You always hear the statement "I am getting 2:1 on my money, and I am very rarely more than a 2:1 dog," the proverbial math call. After you put the table below into your memory, you'll be able to calculate closer calls than you ever have. Now let's take a look at the table for heads-up win percentages against any two random cards. It should be noted that the numbers below reflect your win rate percentage if your opponent is playing 100% of the available hand range. If your opponent is tighter, these numbers do not apply. The numbers are derived from PokerStove.

AA	85%	AKs	67%	KQs	63%	QJs	60%
KK	82%	AQs	66%	KJs	63%	QTs	59%
QQ	80%	AJs	65%	KTs	62%	Q9s	58%
JJ	77%	ATs	65%	K9s	60%	Q8s	56%
TT	75%	A9s	63%	K8s	58%	Q7s	54%
99	72%	A8s	62%	K7s	58%	Q6s	54%
88	69%	A7s	61%	K6s	57%	Q5s	53%
77	66%	A6s	60%	K5s	56%	Q4s	52%

66	63%	A5S	60%	K4S	55%	Q3S	51%
55	60%	A4S	59%	K3S	54%	Q2S	50%
44	57%	A3S	58%	K2S	53%		
33	54%	A2S	57%				
22	50%						
JTS	58%	T9S	54%	98s	51%	87s	48%
J9S	56%	T8S	52%	97s	49%	86s	46%
J8S	54%	T7S	51%	96s	47%	85s	45%
J7S	52%	T6S	49%	95s	46%	84s	43%
J6S	51%	T5S	47%	94s	44%	83s	41%
J5S	50%	T4S	47%	93s	43%	82s	40%
J4S	49%	T3S	46%	92s	42%		
J3S	48%	T2S	45%				
J2S	47%						
76s	45%	65s	43%	54s	41%	43s	39%
75s	44%	64s	41%	53s	40%	42s	37%
74s	42%	63s	40%	52s	38%		
73s	40%	62s	38%			32s	36%
72s	38%						
AK	65%	KQ	61%	QJ	58%	JT	55%
AQ	64%	KJ	61%	QT	57%	J9	53%
AJ	64%	KT	60%	Q9	55%	J8	51%

♥
♣
♦

AT	63%	K9	58%	Q8	54%	J7	50%
A9	61%	K8	56%	Q7	52%	J6	48%
A8	60%	K7	55%	Q6	51%	J5	47%
A7	59%	K6	54%	Q5	50%	J4	46%
A6	58%	K5	53%	Q4	49%	J3	45%
A5	58%	K4	52%	Q3	48%	J2	44%
A4	57%	K3	51%	Q2	47%		
A3	56%	K2	51%				
A2	55%						
T9	52%	98	48%	87	45%	76	42%
T8	50%	97	46%	86	43%	75	41%
T7	48%	96	44%	85	41%	74	39%
T6	46%	95	44%	84	39%	73	37%
T5	44%	94	41%	83	37%	72	35%
T4	44%	93	40%	82	37%		
T3	43%	92	39%				
T2	42%						
65	40%	54	38%	43	35%	32	32%
64	38%	53	36%	42	33%		
63	36%	52	34%				
62	34%						

I have created a simple system for you to calculate in your head the exact odds within one or two percentage points of any two hole cards you are dealt and their win rate heads-up versus any two random cards. Let's start with the pocket pairs. AA is 85%, and 22 is 50%. If you look at the table above, you'll notice that the percentage drops by almost three percent when you start at AA and move down to 22.

So really you have to remember only one number. AA has an 85% win rate against any two random hole cards with a 100% range. If you want to figure out 77, simply count down from AA to 77 (don't count AA as one, count KK as one) and multiply by three percent; then subtract from 85%. So KK is one, QQ is two, and so on until you reach 77, which is seven. Seven times three percent is 21%; simply subtract 21% from 85% and you have your answer: 64%. The actual win rate is 66%, not exact, but do we really care about two percent? You could also count up from 50% and add 15%, which would give you 65%, also very close to the actual number and more than enough information for you in 30 seconds or less at the table. Not only that, but do you think your opponent knows within two percent what her odds are? I doubt it. It's a monster edge.

Now let's move on to AKs and move down to A2s. The only number you will have to recall is 67. AKs has a 67% win rate against any two random hole cards with a 100% range. A2 suited is exactly 10% lower at 57%. Now, if you want to figure out A4s, I would start at 67% (which is AKs) and subtract 10% to get to A2s and count up by one percent each number. So A3s is 58%, A4s is 59%, and you have your answer. The actual number in the table is 59%. If it were ATs, then count down from AKs. AQ, AJ, ATs are three percent, so 67% minus three percent is 64%. The actual number in the table is 65%, very close.

This last system works for any AK to A2 suited or unsuited, KQ to K2 suited or unsuited, QJ to Q2 suited or unsuited, JT to J2 suited or unsuited and T9–T2 suited or unsuited. It is always 10% for all of those. This is where it becomes super easy. For 98 to 92 suited or unsuited, it's nine percent top to bottom; for 87 to 82 suited or unsuited, it's eight percent top to bottom; and for 76 to 72 suited or unsuited, it's seven percent. Now, for the rest — 65 to 62, 54 to 52, 43 to 42, and 32 — simply count down by two percent from the top and you will be fairly close. How do we get all the top numbers? Easy. Start at AKs as 67%. 32s is 36% or 31% lower. Thirty-one divided by 12 hands is almost three percent again! So, if you want the start of 98s, 9 is closer to the Ace than the 3, so count down. K, Q, J, T, and 9. Five times three is 15%, subtracted from 67% is 52%. The actual number is 51%. Now, your bottom is nine percent from 52%, or 43%, and if you want to know 95 suited count down by two percent (not by one percent) because we are in the nines or lower, and you have 44%. The actual number is 46%. Again very close to the number.

As you get to the lower numbers below 876 suited, you'll notice it isn't 10%, mainly because there aren't as many hands. If you want to get even closer, simply subtract about 2% from each hand down from the top and you will be close. Having said that, *are you really calling a desperate all-in with* 85s? Probably not unless you have a tonne of chips and your opponent has no fold equity, but in the interest of being complete, I told you how to remember all the sets of 169 starting hands. Now, interestingly enough, as you move from AKS to KQS, you move from 67% to 63% about three percent all the way down to 32S. In fact, over 11 steps, it's 31% that you lose in win percentage. So it's exactly 2.81% on average. If you round it up to three percent, you give yourself a slightly conservative amount on a win percentage. So, if you want 98s, you simply count down AKQJT9 — five steps down times three percent, about 15% total. Sixty-seven percent minus 15% is approximately 52% — it's actually 51%, close enough to make a decision. You can now take a few moments to calculate in any major tournament, if the person shoves all in UTG, his hand range is 100%, and if you have a hand that gives you a decent win percentage and your chips are large you might want to consider a looser call than you normally would.

Now for unsuited simply start with your new magic number of 65%, two percent lower than our other number for AKS at 67% and repeat.

I think you will find this a simple count-up or -down solution to finding any set of hole cards you have and their approximate win rate against any two random cards.

Another tool I have included is a tight-to-loose scale of hands and the hand that you would need to have at least a 60% chance of winning based on any two random cards in that hand range. For example, if a player plays 35% of her hands and shoves all-in, what is the minimum hand range to have a minimum 60% win rate on any two random hole cards within that player's range? The answer is AA through TT, AK, and AQ suited and AK. These tables memorized will be like a quick reference guide at the poker table. This is especially handy when you are wondering whether or not you should call an all-in from a desperate player with a wider hand range. The difference is that you will know what to do instead of making a wild call and looking it up after — costing you chips. The best part is we have a simple way of deducing this as well through the use of images. The following tables will be converted into images at the end, and it will be a lot easier, but I wanted to illustrate what you will have in your mind.

Player plays 100% of hands

AA	AKS	KQS	QJS	AK	KQ
KK	AQS	KJS		AQ	KJ
QQ	AJS	KTS		AJ	KT
JJ	ATS	K9S		AT	
TT	A9S			A9	
99	A8S			A8	
88	A7S				
77	A6S				
66					
55					

Player plays 95% of hands

AA	AKS	KQS	QJS	AK	KQ
KK	AQS	KJS		AQ	KJ
QQ	AJS	KTS		AJ	
JJ	ATS			AT	
TT	A9S			A9	
99	A8S				
88	A7S				
77					
66					

Player plays 90% of hands

AA	AKS	KQS	AK	KQ	
KK	AQS	KJS	AQ		
QQ	AJS	KTS	AJ		

JJ	ATS		AT		
TT	A9S		A9		
99	A8S				
88	A7S				
77					
66					

Player plays 85% of hands

AA	AKS	KQS	AK	KQ	
KK	AQS	KJS	AQ		
QQ	AJS		AJ		
JJ	ATS		AT		
TT	A9S		A9		
99	A8S				
88					
77					
66					

Player plays 80% of hands

AA	AKS	KQS	AK		
KK	AQS		AQ		
QQ	AJS		AJ		
JJ	ATS		AT		
TT	A9S				
99					
88					
77					

Player plays 75% of hands

AA	AKS	KQS	AK		

KK	AQS		AQ		
QQ	AJS		AJ		
JJ	ATS		AT		
TT	A9S				
99					
88					
77					

Player plays 70% of hands

AA	AKS	AK			
KK	AQS	AQ			
QQ	AJS	AJ			
JJ	ATS	AT			
TT	A9S				
99					
88					

Player plays 65% of hands

AA	AKS	AK			
KK	AQS	AQ			
QQ	AJS	AJ			
JJ	ATS				
TT					
99					
88					

Player plays 60% of hands

AA	AKS	AK			
KK	AQS	AQ			
QQ	AJS	AJ			

♥

♣

♦

JJ	ATS				
TT					
99					
88					

Player plays 55% of hands

AA	AKS	AK			
KK	AQS	AQ			
QQ	AJS	AJ			
JJ	ATS				
TT					
99					
88					

Player plays 50% of hands

AA	AKS	AK			
KK	AQS	AQ			
QQ	AJS				
JJ	ATS				
TT					
99					

Player plays 45% of hands

AA	AKS	AK			
KK	AQS	AQ			
QQ	AJS				
JJ					
TT					
99					

Player plays 40% of hands

AA	AKS	AK			
KK	AQS	AQ			
QQ	AJS				
JJ					
TT					

Player plays 35% of hands

AA	AKS	AK			
KK	AQS				
QQ					
JJ					
TT					

Player plays 30% of hands

AA	AKS	AK			
KK	AQS				
QQ					
JJ					
TT					

Player plays 25% of hands

AA	AKS	AK			
KK	AQS				
QQ					
JJ					

Player plays 20% of hands

AA	AKS	AK			

KK				
QQ				
JJ				

Player plays 15% of hands

AA	AKS	AK		
KK				
QQ				

Player plays 10% of hands

AA				
KK				
QQ				

Player plays 5% of hands

AA				
KK				

So how do we commit this monster amount of information to memory? It's simple. First we determine our minimum hand range requirements for the loosest of loose players. Then we figure out if we have a hand in that range. Next we memorize the minimum percentage played number for each set of hole cards. Then we apply the number to the player's range. If the hole card percentage played number is less than or equal to the player's VPIP and we are okay with a minimum 60% win rate, we call. If it is greater, we fold. For example, a player plays 40% of his hands and shoves all-in on a short stack. We pick up AQ suited. Our AQ suited will give us at least a 60% win rate against a player with a VPIP of 25% or greater; therefore, we call as the player plays 40%. Now let's say we pick up 99. To have the minimum of a 60% win rate against any two random hole cards, we need to have a player who plays 45% or greater of his hands, so in this case we'd fold as our player's VPIP is *less* than 45%. Of course, we have omitted any other information in the hand such as databases and reliable tells; however, with the absence of any other information, this can be used as an excellent guide.

Let's start with the desperate players at 100% hand range. The first table contains all the hands that will give you a maximum 60% win rate against the full range. Below is an easy way to remember it.

> All hands: SPEED LIMIT MULE NUN TOMB SHEET MUMMY
> A nun riding a mule at the speed limit crashes into a
> tomb with a mummy wrapped in a sheet.

Or

> 569J8T: the lowest number in order of each set of cards

Or

> Low jab Jack votes!

Any way you want to remember it is fine.

Below are the percentages of activity for you to be a minimum 60% favorite. The way to use them is simple. If your opponent's activity is greater than the associated percentage, you call; if it is less, you fold, assuming you don't have any other tells or reads on your opponent. This is different from the last set of tables because the VPIP is not 100%. Only four of the sets of hole cards (55, A6S, K9S, and KT) can you play with 100% VPIP. The tighter the player, the less your hand range for that 60% minimum.

AA	Anytime	AKS	15	KQS	75	QJS	95	AK	15	KQ	85
KK	Anytime	AQS	25	KJS	85			AQ	40	KJ	95
QQ	10%	AJS	40	KTS	90			AJ	55	KT	100
JJ	20	ATS	50	K9S	100			AT	70		
TT	30	A9S	70					A9	85		
99	45	A8S	85								

88	55	A7S	90								
77	75	A6S	100								
66	85										
55	100										

So let's review what we have done over the past few chapters. We have our ranks for suited and unsuited hole cards both ranked against full-table play to maximize our chips early in a tournament and heads-up for steal situations later. We can calculate the win percentage of our hole cards against any two other random hole cards heads-up to determine mathematically if a desperate all-in can be called with greater precision, and we have our minimum hole cards with which we can call a shove against a known VPIP activity level from another player. We can easily memorize a positional catalog of hands played by an opponent and easily keep track of her VPIP. Finally, we can determine with a simple word a specific hand range to cross-reference with the VPIP or your positional catalog — all without taking any notes to live play.

Now that you are doing this, admit two things.

1. When you first picked up this book, did you picture yourself ever having the ability to do what is described above? I'm sure you thought it was impossible.

2. The competitive edge you now have isn't just a small percentage. You are now an effective memory machine storing 10 to 100 times the information of your opponents. Isn't it incredible to know that your ability to recall any piece of information by itself or in combination with other pieces of information will utterly destroy your competition and increase your chances of victory by a substantial margin?

Tell me your opponent will be using this information! I guarantee that he will fold hands against people who haven't played hands in "a while" and wonder if his hand is "good enough" to call. You will have exact information and the confidence that you made the correct move, call or fold, which will lower your rate of errors.

Make sure by the end of this chapter that you have all of your 60% win rates versus tight or loose players memorized. Make sure that you memorize all of your win rates against 100% of hands. Know your hands that will give you a minimum 60% win rate against a 100% hand range, 569J8T. Memorize the fact that you subtract three percent for non-suited hands.

EXERCISES

For the following hole cards, count down the percentage win rate versus any two random hole cards within a two percent margin of error.

Hand	
AQ	85
KTS	73S
Q4	62
J7S	99
55	43S

Indicate if you can call the following all-in situations with the following hole cards, assuming you have a minimum 60% win rate in mind.

Player's Playing Percentage	Your Hole Cards	Can You Call, Giving You a 60% Win Rate?
35	99	
80	TT	
100	44	
10	AQS	
70	KQ	
25	A9	

♥
♣
♦

45	AK	
60	A5	
55	QJ	

CHAPTER TM

FROM BLUFFS TO FORMULAS, PUT IT ALL IN YOUR HEAD

In this chapter, we will examine how to memorize common tells and how to memorize person-specific tells, formulas, and other miscellaneous information you can use at the table. By now you must realize the kind of attention you are paying to the table. It will soon become natural to do all the things you have learned in previous chapters as well as capture body language and verbal tells. When you get a reliable tell at a showdown, try to walk yourself through what the player did when he had the top pair or the mid-pair or the absolute nuts. Walk through the betting and try to remember the hand in detail and turn it into images during play, or excuse yourself and write down the particulars until you can memorize them at the break and keep them in your head during play.

We can examine tells and try to turn them into pictures. For this I use examples from the great Mike Caro (see his university website), whom I consider the world's foremost authority when it comes to poker table body language. Let's examine Caro's Law of Tells Number Three: "Any unsophisticated player who bets, then shares his hand while awaiting a call, is unlikely to be bluffing."

So how can we make this an easy way to remember that when a player does this she is strong? Well, one of my favorite characters when I was a boy was Popeye the Sailor. You can use any number of strong superheroes to represent a hand. Superman, the Hulk, and the Thing come to mind.

Whichever you want to use is fine. Let's also look at what an unsophisticated player could be. I use a donkey. Then you need the mind trigger that will help you to instantly see the strong or weak signal in your mind and structure it properly.

SHARING   DONKEY   POPEYE

When you see sharing at the table, you automatically see a donkey. Is the player unsophisticated? If so, you see Popeye, which means strength, and you fold. You have taken an 18-word explanation and turned it into three powerful pictures that tell you exactly what to do or look for.

Let's examine Caro's Number Four: "A trembling bet is a force to be feared." Okay, so trembling means strength, and it happens when the player bets.

BET   TREMBLING   SUPERMAN

So now, if you see a bet and the tremble, you see Superman trembling in fear. Time to fold.

Let's examine Caro's Number Seven: "The friendlier a bettor is, the more apt he is to be bluffing." We have to come up with an image for a lie or bluff or weakness. Pinocchio was a horrible liar. Who is the friendliest guy out there? Maybe the Friendly Giant comes to mind. So, whenever you see the Friendly Giant come to play, picture Pinocchio's nose growing and growing.

FRIENDLY GIANT   PINOCCHIO

That is all you really need to build up your list of images to determine if someone is strong or weak. In fact, one of my exercises was to go through all my poker books on bluffs, strategies, and math to get all of the abstract information into my head once and for all. Imagine having all of your poker books memorized precisely so that you can recall any bit of information you require to call or fold on the thinnest of margins? That is what you have learned so far.

Any tell you pick up at the table can easily be stored using the above method. Simply use strong or weak images to help you store your tells on certain players.

Now let's examine rules from certain players. Todd Brunson has a list of trap hands you can easily memorize in *Power Hold'em Strategy* by Daniel Negreanu. KQ–K9, AJ–A9, QJ–QT, and JT. You can easily come up with an image of a trap and put these hands into it or create a song by which to remember them. You can remember AK and AQ are not trap hands, so remember that if you have 99 dimes you will sink in quicksand. 99TT represents the two 9 hands for A9 and K9 and TT for QT and JT. The quicksand represents the trap.

Negreanu has a rule that an overpair is rarely in the lead after a pot is played all-in on the turn. So maybe you have an image that all-in is a boiling pot of lead and melts bullets. You can create images for betting patterns, bet sizes, check raises — any type of pattern you want.

I am a voracious reader of poker books. In writing this book, I recalled reading parts of *Harrington on Hold'em* that were of particular interest. There are two specific excerpts from the first volume I'd like to touch on. In strategic play, Harrington advocates watching the table and counting how many pots a specific player plays. He says that, if the player is playing one or two pots per round, he is playing conservatively versus three or four pots per round, in which case he is *most likely* playing an aggressive or super-aggressive style. If he is playing more than that, he is giving his money away. With your newly trained VPIP memory technique, and with the greatest of respect to Dan Harrington, you are lightyears ahead of that kind of thinking. You know *exactly* what the range is. He also says that, when a hand is shown down, you should remember key aspects of the hand. Until now, you might not have really known how to remember effectively. I give the quotation below, but I have bolded the parts of the statement I would like to emphasize when it comes to memory training.

> A hand shown down is a gold mine of information. You not only get to see the cards they initially held, **but if you can remember how the hand was bet**, you'll see how they responded to a bunch of different situations. Did they raise or call before the flop? If they raised, how much did they raise? How strong was their hand after the flop, and what did they do with it? Did they slow play a monster, or aggressively bet a weak holding? **The more of this information you can remember the better.**

♥
♣
♦

Notice the emphasis on memory. You can create a complete system of memorization for complete hands shown down. I would also memorize the exact flop, turn, and river cards and the betting on each street. You could also easily remember the blind structure and pot sizes. You could do this for every player, but perhaps you do this with pros only. I think you know by now that, whatever rule you want to keep in your head, you can do it. Make it a funny image and it will always serve to remind you of the correct action. Create your system, and make it simple and organized.

When I first started on my memory quest, my goal was to memorize every hand in order. I quickly found I really didn't need to do this since not a lot of hands are shown down. Create an image for each action, and then use the LOCI method to place all the actions; then, during a break, you can quickly and easily break down the hands and analyze them. Then you can create other images to trigger you into action the next time you see a particular bet. For instance, when I need to remember to take something home from work, I plant a strong emotional image on several places that I will touch when I leave work. When I need to take a certain list home, I plant the list on the doorknob in my office and on the elevator button. I picture my hand getting papercut 1,000 times by my list, and I remember to take it. The same thing will happen when you get check-raised all-in and there is a flush draw on the board. You recall your opponent doing that before with a draw, and you have top pair, so you call; or, you recall your opponent having two pairs, and she plays super scared of flushes. It will trigger you into the correct action as long as you simplify and break down any shown-down hands.

Harrington also goes through varying your raises and using your watch to do it so you throw your opponents off. For AA, KK, QQ, he advocates raising 80% of the time and calling 20% of the time. If your watch's second hand is 48 minutes or less, you raise; if it's in the last 12 minutes, you call. He has a different raise-call ratio for other hands; 88, 77, and 66 use the opposite — 80% calls and 20% raises. He also advocates varying your raise 15% 2x (i.e., 2 times the big blind), 35% 3x, 35% 4x, and 15% 5x the big blind.

I remember reading it and asking myself, "How the heck am I supposed to remember all that?" And that was only two-hand ratios! Now I laugh to myself and wish I had known about memory training before I read that book. It might be a good system, and whether you think it is or not is up to you. What is important is that you can now commit it to memory quickly and easily using images. You will find that the harder work is in discovering your own images to recall the information; once you have them and want to review them, it will take you only minutes to review tons of information before a tournament, and you'll have it all in your head.

Odds memory exercises are easy as well. We can memorize simple pre-flop odds of hitting our hands. For example, if you have a pocket pair, your odds of flopping a set are 11.8% or just shy of 12% or 8.47:1. So you could round up to 9:1 or 12%, and you could have an image of a table where you set 12 place settings representing 12% for a set or take a TRIP with a NINE: your trips are 9:1. Find which odds are important to you and create images for them.

You now know you can use memory aids to recall tells, odds, and how hands are played when they are shown down.

EXERCISES

Go through a book of tells or a book of odds and create images for five different bluffs, five strength hands, and five different odds.

CHAPTER TR
OTHER GAMES

In this chapter, we will look at other games for which we can use memory techniques. It is important to note for the games listed below that you should already have a good if not excellent working knowledge of them. This is not a how-to book but a supplement on key facets to use a highly developed memory as an edge. If you are an expert at the games listed below, you might find my analyses somewhat shallow since my best game is Texas Hold'em. I have played all these games, but I'd be nowhere near the skill level I have in my best game. I haven't covered every poker game out there, but I have put in a few to give examples of how you can use your memory for other types of games. One final note: these are examples; I'm sure you will find many better applications for these techniques and things that work for you in these other games. I would love to hear about it on Facebook. My only goal for this chapter is for you to start thinking about the ways you can store much more information about the game you are playing than your opponent. If that is possible, then my goal will have been achieved.

NON-VISIBLE GAMES:
FIVE-CARD DRAW, BADUGI, AND 2-7 LOWBALL

Draw games turn up very little if any information on the hand until a show-down. They include Five-Card Draw, Badugi, and 2–7 Lowball. In these games, memory can be used to recall VPIP and the cataloging of hands. Because they are draw games, it is difficult to see what the player had before he made his draw (assuming he doesn't stand pat) and therefore more difficult to place him on a hand on the first round of betting. My strategy is to use VPIP to determine his hand ranges and compare them with the added odds of getting dealt specific hands. In a front-loaded game such as 2–7 Lowball, it is also VPIP and showdowns (typically, you can tell if your opponents are drawing to an 8 low or 9 low and what they are calling with). However, in 2–7 Lowball, you can also remember bet sizes to give you the approximate strength of the hand as well as pot sizes for a particular player. Also, when a player stands pat in a single-draw game, there is no guesswork when it comes to his hand. You can easily memorize the hand he had — 98, 97, or 85 — whatever he had.

FIVE-CARD DRAW

This is the first game with no up-cards and no way to determine cards that have been played. There are a few ways you can determine which sets of cards your opponents are playing and whether you can take money from them. We can determine which percentage of hands each player is playing to determine where your chips are going to come from. If we use per-centages from Mike Caro's website (see http://www.caro.com/mcu/tables/Table13.asp), we can illustrate the approximate hand range that a player is playing.

THE PROBABILITY OF BEING DEALT
SPECIFIC HANDS *OR BETTER* BEFORE THE DRAW
(52-card deck – without Joker)

The probability that you will make . . .	Expressed in percent (%) is . . .	The odds against it are . . .	Number of possible combos
Straight Flush	0.00*	64,973 to 1	40
Four-of-a-kind	0.03	3,913 to 1	664
Full House	0.17	589 to 1	4,408
Flush	0.37	272 to 1	9,516
Straight	0.76	131 to 1	19,716
Three-of-a-kind	2.87	33.8 to 1	74,628
Two-Pair	7.63	12.1 to 1	198,180
Pair of A,K,Q,J (Openers)	20.63	3.85 to 1	536,100
Shorts (10's–2's)	49.88	1.00 to 1	1,296,420

*Actually 0.0015%

You can see from this chart that, if the player plays just the standard openers and waits for decent starting hands before the draw, you can expect her to be playing approximately 20% of her hands. We haven't included hands where you are dealt four cards to a straight or flush and other hands. We can assume that those hands represent an additional 10% for a 30% total.

When I tested the numbers, I found the percentage to be approximately 29%. You'll also notice that, if she plays any pair or better, the odds are about 50%, plus the additional hands for 60%. You can use VPIP to determine her hand range based on the chart above. You can also see what she likes to draw to based on her hands being shown down. And you can make mental notes on whether she likes to bet the nuts or check them or if she draws 2 or 3 cards in a single-draw game. You will quickly know where your chips are coming from.

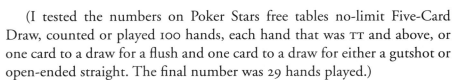

(I tested the numbers on Poker Stars free tables no-limit Five-Card Draw, counted or played 100 hands, each hand that was TT and above, or one card to a draw for a flush and one card to a draw for either a gutshot or open-ended straight. The final number was 29 hands played.)

Here is an *important note*. Poker Tracker has been developed only for Texas Hold'em and Omaha. There isn't a version for any other game. So your own "tracker" in your head will give you a decisive advantage online.

BADUGI

If you aren't familiar with Badugi, it's a fun game to play, but it's a triple-draw limit game, and personally I'm not the biggest fan of limit draw games. If you can't stick all your money in the middle and make your opponent squirm, then most of the fun is gone! Still, many players who play Badugi love it, so in my best effort to apply memory systems to Badugi I have looked up odds tables and determined an adequate VPIP to exploit. I will admit, though, that it is difficult to employ truly amazing techniques in this game, but the best I have come up with is here.

Badugi is a low game like 2–7 Lowball or Razz in that the Ace is a low card and the best low starts with the highest card. You must also have a card from each suit, so AC 2H 3D 4S is the lowest card in Badugi. If you have another suit, the same, or a paired card, you are reduced to a three-card hand.

Because it is a triple-draw game, you see many players gambling it up. VPIP dictates that tight players are playing less than 30% of their hands and looking for starting hands that contain three cards of different suits lower than an 8. If they consistently raise and are drawing one card, most likely you won't gain chips from them. If they limp a lot and draw two or even three cards before the first draw, you might be able to snow them on the last draw or, if you have the best hand, get an extra call from them.

I have also captured some rules and a chart of odds for outs in Badugi. In the charts below, we can create some easy ways to remember the information (see http://www.badugiplayer.com/badugi-odds-chart/).

Take the outs charts, for example. Notice that the outs are almost exactly half of the percentages for one draw. From outs 1 through 5, simply double the outs to get your odds for one draw. From 5 through 10, double the out number and add one percentage point. Easy! One column done. Now, for your next column, multiply your odds by 4 right up to number 10; they are exact up to numbers 6, 7, and 8 subtract 1; 9 and 10 subtract 2 to get your percentage. The final row gets a little tricky. For outs 1 to 3, multiply by 6, then remember this saying — DETAIN A RAILCAP — which stands for 1124579, which in order are the numbers you need to subtract from the 6 multiple. Example: 8 outs 3 times would be 8 x 8 = 48 – 5 (L in RAILCAP), and you have your number: 43%. Now you know how to derive any odds you need in Badugi in a few short steps.

I also got the rules below (edited slightly) from the website. They sounded like good rules to follow and remember in Badugi. It says "note taking," but we are well ahead of that, huh? We can now shove this information into our heads!

NOTE TAKING
Making notes will drastically improve your game; these are some points you should consider.

- Who is misreading his hands or making other very basic mistakes?

- Who doesn't bet or raise until she has a Badugi?

- Who value-bets her good three-card hands?

- Who often folds pre-flop and frequently draws one when he enters a pot? (These players are playing tightly, so proceed with caution.)

- Who limps into a ton of pots and frequently draws one card? (These guys are often drawing to high Badugi.)

- Who has ever been caught in a snow?

- Who has ever tried to pick off a snow: that is, called a river bet versus someone standing pat on earlier rounds?

What you see above is easy to remember. Any player who misreads is green, so you can make him into a green bumbling fool or paint him green in your head. The next one is also easy; when he bets, picture yourself blowing yourself or your chips up. The next player you can picture at Value Village buying second-hand clothing because she is value-betting her three-card hands. You get the picture. Associate each player with a picture and you will quickly and easily get to know your table. By using your odds charts and with the strategy above committed to memory, as well as VPIP, you can raise your odds of winning significantly.

Outs	1 Draw	2 Draws	3 Draws
1	2%	4%	6%
2	4%	8%	12%
3	6%	12%	18%
4	8%	16%	23%
5	10%	20%	29%
6	13%	24%	34%
7	15%	27%	38%
8	17%	31%	43%
9	19%	34%	47%
10	21%	38%	51%

2-7 LOWBALL

For this part, I decided to do the stats on 2–7 NL single-draw game. There is also a triple-draw limit to which you can apply VPIP statistical analysis and draws, but for simplicity I decided to go with the 2–7 single-draw no-limit game.

Kansas City Lowball is another name for this exciting game. Not many people know this, but this game used to decide the best poker player in the world along with Texas Hold'em. Evidently, there was some heated discussions about which would be it, but as we all know Texas Hold'em won out.

When I played 100 hands to get a rough statistical analysis of what a decent player would play, I started out folding everything unless it had four cards under a 10 with a one-card draw for a minimum 10 low. This included hands with possible straight and flush draws that I am sure more seasoned players fold. Of course, in 2–7, an Ace is a high card, and straights and flushes count against you. My number was exactly 30 out of 100 for 30%. Based on how often your opponents play, you can determine if your hand is in the ballpark of being strong enough.

Here are some things to look out for in 2–7 Lowball.

- Call raise move. When a player limps in, there is a three times raise, and then the limper shoves: this is my *call raise* move. In Texas Hold'em, this is almost always indicative of AA or KK; in 2–7 Lowball, it's usually a pat 7 hand, probably the nuts, so be careful.

- Watch the pot size. I found a pretty awesome correlation between pot size and the strength of hand you need. J low and 10 low are usually strong enough only to win limped pots with two to three callers and no betting after the draw. Any higher and you are looking for 8 or maybe even 7 low.

- 2–7 single-draw NL is a pre-draw game. Try to get your money in hard before the draw and force weaker opponents to draw against your pat 9 or 10 hands. Only really bet pat 8s or 7s.

I am not the best 2–7 Lowball player, but these are the few things I did learn playing the game. You can use your memory to recall any piece of information you need to develop. These three game types should get you started.

VISIBLE GAMES:
SEVEN-CARD STUD, RAZZ

I have grouped these games together because the dealing for them is essentially the same.

When I first started doing research for these games, I was intrigued by how many cards you get to see. I did my research not on the high-limit stud game or the low-limit game but on a mid-limit 1–2 game. My research indicated that you can remember from 15 to 20 cards on average that have been played.

So my strategy is this: use VPIP to find the range that a player is playing for a starting hand; then file away using the destruction method the cards that have been played. I would also memorize in order approximately 10 different ways of mutilating or destroying the cards each time a hand is dealt so you don't get confused from hand to hand.

I have included below statistical information (odds from http://www. caro.com/mcu/tables/Table27.asp and http://www.caro.com/mcu/tables/ Table45.asp) to help illustrate a possible hand range for Seven-Card Stud and Razz. From here, we can easily estimate a possible VPIP in both games, and you can adjust accordingly.

THE PROBABILITY OF BEING DEALT SEVEN-STUD STARTING HANDS
(First three cards)

The probability that you will be dealt this on the first three cards . . .	Expressed in percent (%) is . . .	The odds against it are . . .	Number of possible combos
3-Aces	0.02	5,524 to 1	4
3-Jacks through 3-Kings	0.05	1,841 to 1	12
3-Sixes through 3-Tens	0.09	1,104 to 1	20
3-Two's through 3-Fives	0.07	1,380 to 1	16
2-Aces	1.30	75.7 to 1	288
2-Jacks through 2-Kings	3.91	24.6 to 1	864
2-Sixes through 2-Tens	6.52	14.3 to 1	1,440
2-Two's through 2-Fives	5.21	18.2 to 1	1,152
Three parts of a Staight-Flush	1.16	85.3 to 1	256
Three parts of Other Flush	4.02	23.9 to 1	888
Three parts of Other Straight	17.38	4.76 to 1	3,840
ANY Three-of-a-kind	0.24	424 to 1	52
ANY Pair	16.94	4.90 to 1	3,744

3-2-A (Lowest possible)	0.29	344 to 1	64
Four-High or lower	1.16	85.3 to 1	256
Five-High or lower	2.90	33.5 to 1	640
Six-High or lower	5.79	16.3 to 1	1,280
Seven-High or lower	10.14	8.87 to 1	2,240
Eight-High or lower	16.22	5.17 to 1	3,584
Nine-High or lower	24.33	3.11 to 1	5,376
Two parts of a Five-High or lower*	13.76	6.27 to 1	3,040
Two parts of a Six-High or lower*	20.63	3.85 to 1	4,560
Two parts of a Seven-High or lower*	28.89	2.46 to 1	6,384
Two parts of an Eight-High or lower*	38.52	1.60 to 1	8,512

*These starting hands either include a 10-J-Q or K or a PAIR

Now you can see that, in the Seven-Card Stud tables, if your opponent's hand range is any pair, any straight flush, any straight, any flush, or any trips, and if he folds everything else, you can simply add up the percentages to find out a VPIP on him. In this case, it would be a total of 8,780 combinations out of 22,100 combinations, giving you 39.73%. You can commit this number to memory and decide how to play accordingly. Perhaps against this player you wish only to play trips greater than 6, any straight or flush possibility, and pairs greater than Jacks. Your hand range is now 6,172 combinations out of 22,100, giving you a slightly better hand range of 27.93%. If you combine this with the 15–20 cards you'll see in the deck, you should be able to narrow down the hand to a clear winner or loser against you.

With Razz, you can memorize (as with Badugi) the hand ranges you see above. Simplicity, though, is key, so make sure you come up with easy images for each range and know them well. It will be relatively easy to determine where your chips are coming from, especially when you add in the seen cards.

One final note on Seven-Card Stud and Razz: you must know your card images well — meaning you can't be thinking about which image you are trying to destroy. In a full table online, you'll have to destroy seven other cards right off the bat without thinking. It's like becoming fluent in a language versus thinking in English and then translating. You mustn't slow yourself down; it must be done automatically.

GIN RUMMY

I can't talk about memory and Gin Rummy without first sharing some stories about the greatest Gin Rummy player who ever lived: Stu Ungar. Before Stu arguably became the world's greatest no-limit Texas Hold'em tournament player, he was, and I think always will be, the greatest Gin Rummy player. Experts who played the game in his time said he was unbeatable. Legend has it that after four discards he knew every card in your hand — suit and rank. His eidetic memory was the key to his success.

Before Stu, Harry "Yonkie" Stein, a Canadian Gin Rummy player, was widely regarded as the best player of the day. In fact, when they finally played, Stu was listed as a 5:2 underdog to win the match (odds from Nolan Dhalla's *One of a Kind*). Stu took this personally, and they played Hollywood Gin, a variation of rummy with three separate columns for scoring. Over the next four hours, they played 27 games of Hollywood Gin, and Stu completely destroyed the best gin player in the world — winning every game, 81 straight columns. To get games after that, he had to resort to parlour tricks and give huge edges to his competition, such as seeing the bottom card of the deck and always being in the dealer position. Nobody could beat him. In fact, he was asked several times by Las Vegas gin tournaments not to play because several people said they wouldn't play if he were in the tourney. How is that for domination?

In Gin Rummy, you have to use your skills in memorizing cards in order and possibly create a mental image grid to place certain cards in order to narrow down the other person's cards. For example, if you discard a 7 of Spades early and your opponent picks it up, there are several cards she could have. Typically, a good rummy player only picks up cards that complete a meld, so the 7 either completed three 7's or part of a run, 567, 678, or 789 of Spades. Therefore, the red-flag cards you definitely don't want to throw down are any Spade between 4 and 10 and any 7. Knowing which cards have been discarded, you can use the destruction method or put them in sequence.

Sometimes, to throw the other player off, I might throw away a Queen of Hearts and have a 10 and a Jack of Diamonds in the hope that the other player thinks Queens are safe when in reality I need that Queen of Diamonds. You might want to make mental notes about me not to throw away any of these types of cards, knowing they might complete a meld.

The discard pile is also key. Use the destruction method to know which cards have been played to your advantage, and try to nail down what your opponent has early. If need be, you could be like Stu and play defensively.

BRIDGE

Remembering which cards have been discarded and which cards are left in Bridge is the key to success. After some discussion with a friend of mine, Bill Kuz, we decided that this was what I would focus on.

For this exercise, you need to create 13 objects in clockwise order in four rooms in your house using the LOCI method. These 13 objects will be your card denominations. If the first object in your room is a couch, then your couch is the Ace. Each room you have is a designated suit. We will denominate these rooms in Bridge fashion, so the first room is Clubs, the second is Diamonds, the third is Hearts, and the fourth is Spades. So the first room and the first item are for the Ace of Clubs. If it were another item, say the fifth item in the third room, we would descend in order, so the fifth card going down in rank would be AKQJ10. So it would be the 10 of Hearts.

Each time a card is played, use the destruction method to destroy your house item. When it is destroyed, you will easily know after practice what the top-ranked card of each suit is using this method and what has been played. It's also important to note that you should have at least five to 10 ways of mutilating or destroying your items so that you don't get confused on subsequent deals.

For example, if you turned your couch to stone, perhaps on the next deal you inflate it with air and pop it like a balloon; then you could cut it in half with your sword on the next deal. Then you revolve those images and keep your counts.

Any other system you need to remember can be created for an even better system for bidding. Whatever you want to do is possible with your mind; simply create the image and destroy it or save it in a place.

To count your way through a six-deck shoe and reveal the last card, remember the LOCI method for placing your cards in order and mentally review that chapter. Now each room will be a specific number of card. For example, I started off in my living room; now that is my Ace room. My kitchen is my King room, the beige room is my Queen room, my son's room is my Jack room, and so on. Each room has four of your items, to which we are going to add six distinct parts to represent each Ace of Spades, Diamonds, Hearts, and Clubs. In my living room, the first item is my couch, and on it sits six distinct cushions; when each Ace of Spades comes up, I destroy one of the cushions in its place on the couch. The next item is my coffee table. It has the four top corners and the two bottom ones, which I mutilate as each Ace of Diamonds comes up. By the end of the 312 cards, the last cards will stick out like sore thumbs.

Simply go through your existing rooms and, on each item you have in order, designate six spots on the item in clockwise order to be destroyed. Also pick an order for your suits; I use Spades, Diamonds, Hearts, then Clubs. Then work on your speed.

If you don't like that methodology, perhaps you can create different styles of the same images. For example, the Ace of Clubs is a cat. Perhaps you have memorized in order six different types of cats or six different suits. Whatever your system, mutilate it; not only you but also your friends will be impressed.

OMAHA

This is a game for which I really debated whether or not memory could help. Having played the game online, I found that memory techniques could help, but I found that they didn't really help me, mainly because Omaha is a game of the nuts. Also, you really don't bluff the same as you do in Texas Hold'em, and the game is tied more to whether you can take a hand to the river. In fact, you will rarely know opponents' exact hole cards, and you aren't going to get an opponent to fold the nut flush draw or 13-card wrap. For these reasons, I have decided to leave Omaha out of this text.

In summary, you can use memory techniques for almost any card game you want. From Bridge to Razz, you can destroy your opponents by having superior memory skills.

CHAPTER TL
A POKER PLAYER'S ULTIMATE
WEAPON – THE TREADMILL

This might be the most important chapter in this book. If you are going to spend time developing your memory for the great game of poker, consider exercising to keep your brain healthy. I know what you are thinking: "What the hell does physical exercise have to do with what I am doing at the table?" Well, to answer that question, we will look at some recent studies and increase our knowledge of brain function.

Let's look at one of the crucial systems of the brain called the hippocampus. It is responsible for short-term memorization of everything happening right now in your life. It is responsible for taking any immediate memories and transferring what is important and what is not to your long-term memory. That is why, when you study for a test, you can recall most things you have seen right off the bat but might not remember them later because your hippocampus has not transferred them into your long-term memory, deeming them unimportant.

How crucial is this part of the brain? Consider Clive Wearing, an accomplished musician, who contracted viral encephalitis, which normally gives the average person only a cold sore or two. In his case, it attacked his brain, specifically his hippocampus and part of his frontal lobe, responsible for short- and long-term memory storage respectively. The damage to his brain allowed him to remember things only for seven to 30 seconds. In his personal journal, he wrote "I am awake" over and over again and then

♥
♣
♦

crossed it out, realizing that he must have written it before. He remembers little before 1985, he does not remember his children's names, and, though he remembers his second wife, when she leaves the room for more than 30 seconds, he thinks he hasn't seen her in years, and a heartfelt welcome ensues! He also cannot go to the store because he will forget not only where he is going but also where he has come from.

The movie with Adam Sandler and Drew Barrymore called *50 First Dates* is typical of what happens with damage to the hippocampus. She wakes up over and over again not remembering her husband she met and married years ago!

So how can we protect the hippocampus? Exercise. A study conducted by the University of Illinois and the University of Pittsburgh took 120 individuals from 55 to 80 years of age. Half walked for 40 minutes a day, three times a week, and the other half just stretched and did toning exercises. The researchers found that the hippocampus actually increases its volume and increases a person's spatial memory. This won't work for poor Clive because key parts of his brain have been destroyed, but for you it will work, assuming you have a healthy brain. Below is part of the actual document.

> Hippocampal and medial temporal lobe volumes are larger in higher-fit adults, and physical activity training increases hippocampal perfusion, but the extent to which aerobic exercise training can modify hippocampal volume in late adulthood remains unknown. Here we show, in a randomized controlled trial with 120 older adults, that aerobic exercise training increases the size of the anterior hippocampus, leading to improvements in spatial memory.

This is just one study confirming that exercise is healthy for your brain and actually improves memory function. Also, many studies confirm that, when you exercise, your heart rate increases, and that in turn increases overall blood flow to all areas of your body, including your brain.

In short, the next time you are in a tournament for big money, take a brisk walk to get your blood flow up and increase your brain power. It might mean the difference between a shot at a bracelet and finishing somewhere in the top quartile. As well, the best part of keeping in shape is that you will have many years of exceptional health to play poker and make better life decisions. Be sure to exercise regularly.

CHAPTER T SH/CH

FINAL THOUGHTS

I want to thank you for taking this journey with me through a small town in the memory world. If you read this book from cover to cover and didn't do the exercises, then I'd encourage you at this point to go back and reread and study each chapter. Don't get overwhelmed. Training your memory is a process that can take weeks or months. It does take time. Once you have the foundation built, you will see how truly easy it is to commit anything to memory. There is a saying that, if you want to form a new habit or learn something new, it takes about three weeks to start to get good at it. I can see this book being one of the most important you ever study, not just for the game of Texas Hold'em but also for your life.

I would also encourage you to become friends with me on Facebook and follow me on Twitter (@bennettonika) and let me know how this book has impacted your game. I look forward to hearing from you. I will endeavor, of course, to respond to any questions asked of me and try to help out. It will be my small thanks to you for purchasing my book.

In the meantime, go and find a live game — and *annihilate it*!

ANSWERS
TO EXERCISES

CHAPTER N

1. Your brain thinks in pictures.
   4 942 70 2 97140
2. You have one hundred billion neurons.
   8 2 2141 952 2420
3. Train your memory every day.
   142 4 334 84 1
4. You have a super memory.
   8 094 334
5. I can memorize a shuffled deck of cards in order.
   72 3340 6851 17 8 7410 2 414
6. 4581
   RELIVED
7. 267
   NEW SHACK
8. 9364
   BOMB CHAIR

9. 1548

> **DOLLAR FEE**

10. 7632

> **CASH MAN**

CHAPTER M

1	DOCK	7D
2	HIGH DOME	KH
3	SOCK	7S
4	COFFEE	8C
5	CAR	4C
6	COMB	3C
7	HARE	4H
8	HAY TEN	QH
9	HUT	AH
10	DEAN	2D
11	CANE	2C
12	DIME	3D
13	STEM	KS
14	COTTON	QC
15	HAM	3H
16	DAYTONA	QD
17	SOAP	9S
18	CADET	JC
19	SUIT	AS

1	3H	HAM
2	2C	CANE
3	7S	SOCK
4	9D	DIAPER
5	8C	COFFEE
6	QC	COTTON
7	AC	CAT
8	2H	HEN
9	TD	DICE
10	3D	DIME
11	7D	DOCK
12	TC	CASE
13	QD	DAYTONA
14	6D	DISH
15	9C	COP
16	8D	DIVE
17	9S	SOAP
18	KD	DAYTIMER
19	QS	STAIN

20	SUN	2S		20	JS	STEED
21	DIET	AD		21	3C	COMB
22	COAL	5C		22	2S	SUN
23	DAYTIMER	KD		23	5S	SAIL
24	SAUCE	TS		24	5H	HAIL
25	CASH	6C		25	4H	HARE
26	HOOK	7H		26	9H	HOOP
27	HITCH	6H		27	JH	HOT TEA
28	COAL	5C		28	AD	DIET
29	HOT TEA	JH		29	KS	STEM
30	SUSHI	6S		30	2D	DEAN
31	DIVE	8D		31	8H	HIVE
32	HEN	2H		32	7H	HOOK
33	DOOR	4D		33	5D	DOLL
34	SUMO	3S		34	5C	COAL
35	SOUR (GRAPES)	4S		35	6C	CASH
36	DOLL	5D		36	4C	CAR
37	COP	9C		37	TS	SAUCE
38	DIAPER	9D		38	6H	HITCH
39	DICE	TD		39	4S	SOUR (GRAPES)
40	CAT	AC		40	7C	CAKE
41	DISH	6D		41	3S	SUMO
42	HOSE	TH		42	JC	CADET
43	HOOP	9H		43	4D	DOOR
44	CAKE	7C		44	QH	HAY TEN

45	SOFA	8s
46	HIVE	8H
47	DOTTED	JD
48	CUT ME (*Rocky*)	KC
49	STEED	JS
50	STAIN	QS
51	HAIL	5H
52	CASE	TC

45	6s	SUSHI
46	JD	DOTTED
47	TH	HOSE
48	KC	CUT ME (*Rocky*)
49	8s	SOFA
50	KH	HIGH DOME
51	AH	HUT
52	AS	SUIT

CHAPTER R

1	2	3
TC	7C	2C
JC	8C	JC
QC	QC	2D
KC	4D	6D
JD	5D	7D
8H	JD	7H
9H	AH	AS
4S	2H	9S
6S	QS	TS
TS	KS	KS

CHAPTER SH, CH, OR J

86	FISH	TOOTED	111
90	BUS	TOMATO	131
137	DIM MAK	TATER (TOT)	114
168	TWO SHIV(S)	RYE	4
88	FIFE	TOONS	120
132	DEMON	DOODLE	115
140	DRESS	FIB	89
49	ROPE	TRAP	149
6	SHOE	MOVIE	38
96	BEACH	DUMP	139
24	NERO	CHAIN	62
45	ROLL	TRASH	146
39	MOP	CAKE	77
116	TOT SHOE	DIET C(OKE)	117
156	TOOL CH(EST)	LANE	52
70	KISS	TAILOR	154
3	MU	PUFF	98
22	NUN	TIE TUB(ES)	119
83	FOAM	TEST	101
69	SHIP	CASH	76
91	BAT	TIE CHOK(ING)	167
13	TOMB	SHEET	61
35	MULE	RAKE	47

144	TERROR	CHERRY	64
152	TALON	FIRE	84
169	TOSHIBA	DASH	16
51	LOT	DISH L(ADY)	165
138	DMV	NET	21
40	RICE	FOZZIE	80
104	TASER	TUMS	130

CHAPTER HARD C OR K

76	UNION OIL	KING COBRA	K7
K6	KICKS	QUEEN LATIFAH IN BED	Q6
QT	QUENTIN TARANTINO	COMPUTER	Q7
74	DOUBLE DOWN	KNIVES	K5
88	SNOWMEN	JOHNNY MOSS	AT
44	SAILBOATS	HECKLE AND JECKLE	J2
Q4	HOUSEWORK	SIEGFRIED AND ROY	QQ
97	STU UNGAR	KATE	K8
43	BOOK	HOUSEWORK	Q4
K9	CANINE	BLOCKY	63
AJ	BLACKJACK	DOLLY PARTON	95
73	DUTCH WAITER	FISH HOOKS	JJ

T5	WOOLWORTH'S	KUWAIT	Q8
A2	HUNTING SEASON	QUARTER	52
JT	JUSTIN TIMBERLAKE	MOTOWN	J5
92	TWIGGY	VODKA	62
A8	DEAD MAN'S HAND	DAISY DUCK	Q2
TT	DIMES	ROUTE 66	66
QJ	MAVERICK	SPLIT	T7
T2	DOYLE BRUNSON	BULLY JOHNSON	53

CHAPTER F

	RANK 9–10	**RANK HU**
76s	66	115
K6	106	62
QT	36	47
74s	103	134
88	23	7
44	71	48
Q4s	70	76
97	112	109
43	154	164
K9s	22	29
AJ	21	15

73S	120	143
T5S	98	106
A2	101	59
JTS	18	45
92S	121	132
A8	61	32
TT	7	5
QJ	28	38
T2S	109	118
K7S	44	44
Q6	125	81
Q7S	53	61
K5S	49	54
AT	30	19
J2	153	122
QQ	3	3
K8	84	51
Q4	137	93
63S	110	147
95S	96	113
JJ	4	4
Q8	94	68
52	160	166
J5S	82	91
62S	127	156

Q2	145	105
66	48	17
T7	114	101
53S	99	146

CHAPTER B

Seat	VPIP (%)
1	40
2	20
3	20
4	30
5	50
6	70
7	60
8	50
9	70

CHAPTER TS

Button	Seat	Position	Pre-Flop	SHDWN	
B	1	9	F		
SB	2	1	F		
BB	3	2	F		
	4	3	F		

	5	4	F		
	6	5	F		
	7	6	R	AKS	red law symbol in the tree trunk
	8	7	C	AQ	yellow towels on players
	9	8	C	77	yellow rice on stage
	1	8	F		
B	2	9	F		
SB	3	1	F		
BB	4	2	F		
	5	3	F		
	6	4	R/C	JTS	red dive in a shark's mouth
	7	5	R	KQ	red tub on the branch
	8	6	F		
	9	7	F		
	1	7	F		
	2	8	F		
B	3	9	C	89	yellow bus in the pool
SB	4	1	C	55	yellow chain in the lineup

BB	5	2	C	A2	yellow test on the headlights
	6	3	R	ATS	red tin stuck in the shark's eyes
	7	4	F		
	8	5	F		
	9	6	F		
	1	6	F		
	2	7	F		
	3	8	R	A9S	red nose on the back door
B	4	9	F		
SB	5	1	C	J9	yellow cherry on the bumper
BB	6	2	C	54	yellow DMV in the shark's nostril
	7	3	F		
	8	4	F		
	9	5	F		
	1	5	R	QQ	red MU on the bell
	2	6	F		
	3	7	F		
	4	8	C	T9S	yellow neck on the splash

B	5	9	C	AQ	yellow towel on the exhaust pipe
SB	6	1	F		
BB	7	2	C	AA	yellow tie on the lights
	8	3	F		
	9	4	F		
	1	4	F		
	2	5	F		
	3	6	F		
	4	7	F		
	5	8	F		
B	6	9	R	J8s	red roll on the dorsal fin
SB	7	1	F		
BB	8	2	C	A4	yellow Fozzie Bear in the entrance
	9	3	F		
	1	3	F		
	2	4	F		
	3	5	F		
	4	6	R	88	red gnome on the climb

	5	7	C	KTS	yellow tire on the tail lights
	6	8	C	QJ	yellow knife in the pectoral fin
B	7	9	F		
SB	8	1	F		
BB	9	2	F		
BB	1	2	C	T2S	yellow teaspoon on the smokebox
	2	3	F		
	3	4	F		
	4	5	F		
	5	6	F		
	6	7	F		
	7	8	F		
B	8	9	F		
SB	9	1	R	84	red tool chest on John
SB	1	1	C	34	yellow tailor on the railguard
BB	2	2	C	86s	yellow chef in the glove
	3	3	F		
	4	4	F		

♠
♥
♣

	5	5	R	AK	red toes on the roof
	6	6	F		
	7	7	F		
	8	8	F		
B	9	9	C	JJ	yellow rye on the audience
B	1	9	C	74S	yellow tisma on the rail
SB	2	1	C	AJS	yellow bee on the left pad
BB	3	2	C	Q4	yellow dim mak kills the garage
	4	3	F		
	5	4	F		
	6	5	F		
	7	6	F		
	8	7	F		
	9	8	R	TT	red cow on stage

Hand Counts

1	4	6	5
2	2	7	3
3	3	8	2
4	3	9	4
5	5		

CHAPTER TT

%	% Image	# Image	Range Image	#	Pairs	Suited	Unsuited
20	NOSE	MIR	V BADGE	34	88	9	J
40	RICE	CHIVE	LOW QUEEN CAB	68	55	AKQ–7	9
35	MULE	LOBE	CHOKING COP	59	66	AK–7	9
80	FOZZIE	TWO MOLE(S)	AA QUEEN CHIA	135	ANY	ANY	AKQ–6
10	TOES	TICK	BOUTIQUE	17	99	T	Q

CHAPTER TN

Hand	Count (%)	Actual (%)
AQ	64	64
KTS	61	62
Q4	51	52
J7S	53	52
55	59	60
85	43	41
73S	41	40
62	35	34
99	70	72
43S	37	39

Player's Playing Percentage	Your Hole Cards	Can You Call, Giving You a 60% Win Rate?
35	99	N
80	TT	Y
100	44	N
10	AQS	N
70	KQ	N
25	A9	N
45	AK	Y
60	A5	N
55	QJ	N

ACKNOWLEDGMENTS

I would like to thank the people who have helped me on this wonderful journey to the publication of this book.

To My Family

To my kids Bennett and Onika, I thank you for the use of your names and this book is dedicated to you both, my pride and joy. Every day you make me a very proud and happy father, and I love you both very much. To my wife, Leissa, I love you more than anything and without your complete and unwavering support at home this book could not have been written.

To Keith Strong, thank you for providing your insights and opinions for the title of the book. Without you, the title would have been *secret* instead of *hidden*!

To ECW Press

Jack, a personal thanks for believing in my ideas and my book; save my kids and family, having someone like you fond enough of my manuscript to publish it is the best feeling a person can have.

A special thanks to Dallas Harrison, Erin Creasey, Rachel Ironstone, Troy Cunningham, Dee Hopkins, and Crissy Boylan for making my book look awesome and more importantly making me sound incredible. Your team has been nothing but the most professional and even though at times it seemed we were jousting, in the end I truly feel the best decisions that could have been made were made. I enjoyed working with all of you.

I would also like to thank Alexis Van Straten, my publicist, for her drive to promote and sell my work as well as keep my excitement down so we could get the buzz going at the right time!

I would also like to thank my friend at Sisler High School Bill Kuz for his insights and knowledge of bridge.

I would also like to thank Rick Best, Steven Brennan, and Brian Bowman for keeping me safe.

To the Pro Poker Players

Thank you for taking the time to talk to me in Las Vegas in 2011. I know it must have seemed odd to have this huge guy handing his manuscript to you in between breaks at the WSOP, but I really do thank you for listening and providing testimonials.

To my Poker League in Winnipeg

Thank you for coming out each month and letting me test my systems out. Many of the systems in the book were created and fine-tuned at the tables against you during the 2010–2011 season. I would like to especially thank Will Hall and Paul Tomlinson for proofreading and providing me with constructive criticism, as well as David Moscovitch for relentlessly going after testimonials in Las Vegas. I would also like to thank specific members in the league for sharing their poker stories in this book, particularly Adam Terwin, Marc Virgo, and Sean Brooks. I would also like to thank Polly Hewson, Mark Cohn, Mark Hart, Bryan Boyle, Marc Virgo, Bill Ladyman, Dave Moscovitch, Will Hall, Anders Prokopowich, Jon Hanec, Mark Braun, Jason Braun, Jack Sutton, Will Clarke, Roy Mulchand, Livio Foianesi, and Chris Thiessen for giving me positive feedback and filling me with even more confidence that my ideas were good.